Lara McKenzie, with a BSc in Business, has worked as a management consultant for international companies in different countries throughout her twenties and thirties until she was diagnosed with Schizophrenia in 2012. This is her first published work, a memoir, and describes her life journey along with her descent into mental illness and her dedication to recovery. Lara lives in Surrey, United Kingdom.

For justice.

This book is a short memoir. It reflects the author's present recollections of experiences over her lifetime. Names and identifying details have been changed to protect the privacy and anonymity of individuals, and many events have been compressed, and some dialogue has been recreated.

WITHOUT PREJUDICE

Lara McKenzie

VIRTUAL INSANITY

AUSTIN MACAULEY PUBLISHERS™

LONDON • CAMBRIDGE • NEW YORK • SHARJAH

A CIP catalogue record for this title is available from the British Library.

ISBN 9781528976602 (Paperback)
ISBN 9781528976619 (Hardback)
ISBN 9781528976640 (ePub e-book)

www.austinmacauley.com

First Published (2020)
Austin Macauley Publishers Ltd
25 Canada Square
Canary Wharf
London
E14 5LQ

When I stand before God at the end of my life, I would hope that I would not have a single bit of talent left, and could say, "I used everything you gave me."

Emma Bombeck

Prologue

It's February 2018 and I am very sick.

They are injecting me now. I watch the mental health nurse prepare the Zyprexa (Olanzapine) solution which comes in a bright yellow powder form. She delicately inserts the needle into the saline solution and then inserts it into the yellow powder vile releasing the fluid. Then she swirls the vile around and around making sure all the powder of the drug becomes liquid. I watch her extract 300mg of Zyprexa into the syringe. She asks me to lie on my side as she uses her hand to identify the spot she wants to inject into. "Sharp scratch," she says to me, as she inserts the needle into my side and injects the liquid drug. After she has finished, she asks me to wait in reception. I must be monitored for two hours after each injection; Zyprexa can affect one's blood pressure. So, I sit with a cup of tea, and wait. My injection is every fortnight.

I was first diagnosed with Schizophrenia in 2012 at the age of 36, and it's known as a late-onset diagnosis. It would not be my last diagnosis, and in both Australia and the UK they have kept changing my diagnosis over the years. Finally, in 2017, I was diagnosed with Schizoaffective Disorder.

Zyprexa has made me put on a lot of weight. Spending most of my adult life at 54kg, I am now 86kg. I have a bulging stomach that makes me feel like I am nine months pregnant. I cannot wear high heels anymore as I feel so unbalanced and shaky. Finding a job and keeping a job seems to me to be becoming impossible.

When I'm sick with my symptoms it's hard. I find this to be a debilitating illness. My medications do not cure me. They do not stop my anxiety, depression or Schizophrenia. But they greatly lessen the symptoms, but sometimes they continue. The auditory hallucinations that is. Sometimes daily. Nasty voices swimming from the front of my head calling me a delusional cunt, a schizophrenic whore, there will never be any justice, Jewish whore, drink bitch, we control you bitch, ignore (which is said all day long) and, spastic bitch. I also have what I call good voices, ones that tell I am loved. To keep going and to never give up.

In my current delusions and paranoia, I keep telling myself that the voices are coming from a brain machine interface (brain chip) that I believe was installed in my forehead at a Hospital in England by intelligence agencies. I tell my Psychiatrists these deluded thoughts. They calmly talk to me and tell me that it's a delusion and I have Schizoaffective Disorder. They ask me to use CBT (Cognitive Behavioural Therapy) on myself and these delusions.

The psychiatrists will not give me an x-ray and show the x-ray results to me to prove that the brain chip isn't there; although intelligence agencies would probably make the doctor's give me x-ray results that are not mine. I feel many in the world have lied to me and I do not know why the doctors protect them. But I know that's a delusion too. I guess I want an x-ray, so I have the evidence to prove to myself there is nothing there, that no brain chip is there. To CBT myself. It's so frustrating having a delusion about a brain chip.

As defined in Wikipedia, "The word schizophrenia—which translates roughly as 'splitting of the mind' and comes from the Greek roots schizein (to split) and phren (mind)—was coined by Eugen Bleuler in 1908 and was intended to describe the separation of function between personality, thinking, memory, and perception."

The more I research and reflect on my mental health disorder the more I realise, along with the research that's been done, that it's caused by genetics and environmental factors. Some of the research has shown that it occurs at conception and is a form of spontaneous genetic mutation that further occurs in foetal development. In one study conducted by Doctor Mary-Claire King of the University of Washington in Seattle in 2013, Schizophrenia was found to have genetic spontaneous mutations found in people whose fathers were 33-45 at the time of conception. But my father was 29 when he conceived me, so I don't fit that profile. What is more interesting, however, is that the study identified 'fifty-four genes with spontaneous mutations causing damage to the function of the protein they encode in the prefrontal cortex'. Moreover, fifty of these genes are active during foetal development. Suffice to say, the study supports the theory that in part, Schizophrenia results from disruptions in genetic development during the foetal development in the womb and these genetic mutations cause Schizophrenia.[1] These genetic mutations are not the single cause alone. Environmental factors play a significant role.

I have a permanent, enduring and lifelong brain disorder called Schizoaffective Disorder. It is said to been seen in about 0.5% to 0.8% of the population (Diagnostic and Statistical Manual of Mental Disorders, 4th Edition). I have a higher risk profile for developing dementia in later life, which is something I don't want; lying in a bed not knowing who the hell anybody is. Basically, Schizoaffective Disorder means you can have bi-polar or depressive disorder along with Schizophrenia. I've been diagnosed as Schizoaffective, depressive type. I also suffer from substance abuse (namely tobacco and alcohol) or alcoholism although I go to Alcoholics Anonymous to manage my addictions, even though I have gone in and out of AA like a yoyo. Some days it is pure hell to live with this brain disorder. As some of the studies show, this occurred at conception; I was destined for this mental illness. I had no choice. It's not my fault. I was born with it.

My mental health has cost me a lot. The most significant and painful thing being the loss of my children. In one of my friend's emails to me she said she understands why everyone hates me. The mental health stigma really does exist. I have not seen my children in four years. I have not Skyped with them in two years. I have not seen a photo of them both in nearly two years. I miss my children dearly.

I want to write this book about my life and journey with this severe brain disorder. I want you to see what it's like to see the world and the universe through my eyes and to hopefully reduce some of the stigma around mental health. I am not dangerous or

---

[1]US Department of Health and Human Services https://www.nih.gov/news-events/nih-research-matters/mutated-genes-schizophrenia-map-brain-networks

scary, just different. I also want to track and write my journey into recovery.

You will read this and think at times, she's insane. Yes. It will include delusions about spies and intelligence agencies, people who I thought were VIPs, PSYOPs by militaries, and Illuminati Wizards, just to name a few. Moreover, it would create, what I believe to be, a crisis, if what happened went public in Australia, the USA and the UK. Why I became a part of that, let alone the terrorisation of me, is beyond my comprehension. But I have to remind myself, that's a delusion too.

But that's been my journey and that makes up part of my story. I will talk of the astral field, astral sex (and astral rape) and spirit projection. Also, I want to talk about my severe delusions. Things like what psychiatrists call phantom pregnancies, the Australian Republican Movement and *Star Wars*, being projected into a space telescope by what I thought was a space agency, being gang raped in the astral field with body possessions from Illuminati Wizards saying, "Is it Lucifer?" Moreover, other things like a brain machine interface/ brain chip that I deluded myself into believing was illegally and unlawfully installed in my forehead in the UK, vaginal and abdominal pulling and episodes of suicide; I even emailed the End of Life Clinic in The Netherlands because they have a Euthanasia Act for mental health. There will be some sexual references and sexual talk too.

Psychiatrists refer to my experiences as delusions, hallucinations, voices and paranoia. To me, when I was ill, they were real, and they really happened and that is the difference between me with this brain disorder that I have been diagnosed with and all of you mentally healthy people.

There is a part of me at the moment that wants justice. That wants an explanation. But I have nothing left to obtain justice other than perhaps from governments scrutiny and oversight committees. I can only believe that they want to know the truth and that when their intelligence agencies, military or their allies get out of hand, they need to know. For, they are not provided this information at present. After the International Criminal Court emailed me that they will not take my case, I am resounded to the United States and Australia to uphold my privacy, human rights and self-determination. I believe that people should know if Governments or their agencies get out of hand. Well that's just my opinion anyway. But here I am in my delusions again. Why intelligence agencies chose me I don't know, but I would like to know in particular, why they illegally and unlawfully inserted a military grade brain machine interface in my forehead. But, as psychiatrists say, and I have to remind myself, that's a delusion.

In 2010, whilst I was working for a company in Sydney, a colleague told me in a meeting with him that 'The only way to justice Lara is to write a book'. I started to learn then that many people knew what was happening to me, and no one would tell me the truth.

But more importantly, to me in 2010, I started to feel that my mental health was deteriorating. That my mind was splitting, and I thought to myself, I may have Schizophrenia. And I felt terrified.

So, to those people who said to me I need justice, here is the book.

This is my story.

Chapter One
The Beginnings

I was born on the 15th of November 1975 in Brisbane, Australia when the jacaranda trees with their purple flowers were in full bloom, covering the footpaths and gardens like a soft blanket. Those trees are one of my most favourite memories of my childhood and somehow it felt special to me that they would be in full bloom in November each year. I was born the fourth child to my parents and have three older brothers. My parents told me I was unexpected. They were about to adopt a little girl, but my mother fell pregnant with me and they didn't adopt that little girl. I hope she was adopted by a lovely family.

It's hard to remember back to my early years. I remember living in Melbourne at the age of four and five and visiting an Australian Military base with my mum and brother. We went there to the army barracks where my uncle was serving in the Australian Army. I remember this quite clearly as we went into one of the army tanks and to this day there are photos of that visit.

We moved around a bit from Brisbane to Melbourne and back to Brisbane where at the age of five I started primary school. My holidays were filled with riding my bike down the streets and to the park and going to the Gold Coast and Sunshine Coast to visit my grandparents. I would also go and stay with my grandmother, my dad's mother, which I loved as she would make the best pikelets in town. Often, I would play in my bedroom in Kitchener Road in Ascot; a house that was painted pink and I felt slightly embarrassed about as we were the only pink house in the neighbourhood. I was a bit of a tomboy as a child as I wore t-shirts, shorts and bare feet. I hated wearing dresses; especially pink ones.

I guess what is significant about all of this is that, when I was six years old, I had my first out-of-body (OBE) experience or what they call soul travel or astral projection. Not that I would understand that this is what I was doing at that age.

At night, I would lie in my bed in Kitchener Road and feel my spirit leave my body; I felt like I was flying down Kitchener Road and around the suburb of Ascot. I was six years old when I started doing this. At times I would do it whilst I was sleeping, and it would wake me up as I would do it spontaneously. To me, I thought I was an angel flying around Brisbane with my spirit.

For those of you who do not understand this, it is called astral projection or astral travel (soul travel). Astral travel is a wilful or enforced out-of-body (OBE) experience. To believe this you must believe in the existence of a spirit (soul) or consciousness which is called the astral body. It is separate from our physical body. This astral body (soul and consciousness) has the capability of travelling out of our physical body, into another body and throughout the universe.[2] You can always look at Wikipedia for an explanation. This is important to understand as in my delusions when I was older, I thought this is what intelligence agencies, the Illuminati Wizards and even ISIL (Islamic State of Iraq and the Levant) can do. I also deluded myself into believing this is why sometimes we have some of these terrorist attacks in our countries. But I will come to that much later.

What's important is that I think fathers and mothers, true intelligence agents, true militaries, police forces and the International Criminal Court and Federal/ High Court Justice Systems in each country have a much bigger role to play in protecting children and civilians from the dangers of the astral field, body possessions and crimes against humanity. Currently, it seems the justice system and international justice system does not provide investigation, prosecution and justice for what happens to a person when they are forced and enslaved in the astral field. In truth, protecting us from the Wizards and Illuminati militaries, political leaders and intelligence agencies. On top of this is the psywar on civilians that they engage in and in my delusions, did on me much later in my adult life.

---

[2] https://en.wikipedia.org/wiki/Astral_projection

Regardless, as a child, I loved to astral travel at night in my room and it felt like I was flying around Brisbane. But to me, and what I believe, is that someone found out I was doing this as many spies stay for long periods of time in the astral field. I believe they found out I was doing this. I do not know who but to me it was a spy or an Illuminati Wizard. It stopped then, as I felt (what I now know are the Wizards and Illuminati) someone projecting himself/themselves on the black and white tiles outside me bedroom. Soon after this I would have my first anxiety attack although at the time, I did not know it was anxiety I was experiencing; that has only come with hindsight. I would spend decades to come suffering from anxiety.

Other aspects of my childhood that I remember is my love to dress up and dance as a child and put on little dance shows for my friend's parents when I would stay over at a friend's house. Moreover, I would play Fleetwood Mac's song *Seven Wonders* and I would think that I was talking a Light Force alien called Paul. Decades later, Paul would visit me time and time again and make me laugh so much. But I will get to that later. Suffice to say, I guess my mental health wasn't that great as a child either.

I also went to the Anglican Church and Sunday School at church which was down the road from where we lived in Ascot. I used to ride my bike down to church each Sunday, feeling rather confused about religion but still enjoying my Sunday School lessons. One day in Sunday School, I found, or I wrote (I cannot remember) some swear words written in the back of the Bible. I remember the Sunday School teacher talking about it, but I do not know if it was me. It was significant to me because I was shocked at it and questioned why it was written in the back of the Bible. I often thought about God during these times particularly thoughts like, why am I here? However, most of my life I have turned to God for solace.

Part of the teachings I think I received at Sunday School (or I otherwise somehow came up with myself) was about Lucifer and I was taught, as later Christian teachings went, that he was a male angel who was the Devil as he had fallen from God's Grace. In Dante's Inferno (the late Italian poet of the late Middle Ages), Lucifer is the fallen angel and king of hell. Little did I know that this concept of Lucifer would come back into my life in the most unfathomable way possible decades later.

In some ways, during these years of childhood, I would question God and blame him for some of the things that were happening to me. It would be a decade later until I would learn about 'free will' and that it was not God's doing.

During these years, there were some significant behaviours that I got myself into and others where I was just a victim. I started smoking cigarettes. In those days, the early 1980s, you could go down to the corner store in Ascot, Brisbane and buy a packet of cigarettes and just say to the shop assistant, "I'm buying them for my parents," and they would sell them to you. I thought that was fantastic. I would then ride my bike to the park and smoke them, using matches to light them. When I did this, I also saw Indigenous Australians sleeping in the park and used to offer them a cigarette. I thought I was very cool getting away with this.

When I was eight to ten years old, we often had governesses as my dad and mum would travel overseas for months at a time for my dad's work. One of the governesses also smoked so I used to steal a cigarette or two from her packet on the bench and go underneath the big old Queenslander house we had and smoke them. Once I went to boarding school when I was eleven, this all stopped. But I would pick up smoking again when I was eighteen years old at university and I still struggle with it to this day. Both my mum's mother, Nanine, and my step-grandfather, Pop, smoked cigarettes. Both died of lung cancer when I was around nine years old.

From these trips overseas that my dad and mum went on they would always bring me back little gifts from the UK and what I remember to be Russian Matryoshka dolls. I loved them.

I also had my first taste of alcohol when I was about eight or nine. Sometimes I would taste the leftovers in the wine glasses that were left after one of my parent's parties. Other times one of my St Margaret's school friends would get wine coolers and we would drink them at her house. Little did I know alcohol would become an issue for me later in my life and something I would have to address repeatedly.

I remember we used to sing *God Save the Queen* at my first primary school in Grade 1, every morning before classes began. I would stand and sing this anthem at the time and loved to bellow out the part of the anthem, "Send her victorious, happy and glorious bound to reign over us." I particularly enjoyed singing this anthem and loved the words 'send her victorious'. However, this changed at my school when in 1981 the Australian National Anthem was introduced which I remember having to sing. I mention this because decades later, I had severe delusions that the Australian Republican Movement, along with militaries and intelligence agencies, would enter my life and involve me in what I deluded myself to believe was a silent war on Australia becoming a Republic. In the UK, when I was living there in 2016, I would remember singing *God Save the Queen* as a child and sing it out aloud in my living room in Godalming in the UK.

I felt very close to my grandparents when I was a child and, when both my grandmothers died, it had a significant emotional impact on me. My dad's mum, Grandma asked me to come and see her in hospital just before she died, and I remember it very clearly holding her hand. She died of heart disease. I never knew my grandfather (my dad's father) as he died when Dad was 21 years old. After I had lost my grandmothers and Pop, my step-grandfather, I remember sitting on my bed in Kitchener Road in Ascot crying and feeling their presence, like they were somehow near me and trying to communicate with me. My dad came into my room and saw me crying and said, "What's wrong? Why are you crying?" I explained I missed my grandmothers and tried to tell him that I feel them. He said, "They are dead, Lara. I know it's hard, but they have gone."

My mum's dad, Granddad, I was very fond of and he lived until 2010. He served in the Royal Australian Army during World War II in Syria against the Nazis and Vichy French and in Asia against the Japanese. When I was a child, I would spend my school holidays with him, and my step-grandmother and Granddad showed me some of the items (war trophies) he collected. Little did I know that the conversations with him about World War II would become a significant part of my interest in history and later in my life and in my delusions, a significant part of my journey with the Illuminati Wizards.

I had some other strange behaviours as a child along with quite a bit of trouble at school. I started at a government State School but ended up being moved to a private girls' school in Brisbane. But I struggled making friends at school. Social cues I could not grasp well and many of the girls at this private girls' school turned against me and I had no friends for some of the years I was there. I remember this impacting me somewhat as my mother would always pack pears and apples in my school bag and I would leave them in the bottom of my bag for weeks on end until they smelt and rotted. I do not know why I did this. I struggled academically at school and my grades were always poor getting Cs and Ds most of the time. This academic pattern continued well into my teenage years until I went to a prestigious girls' boarding school in the UK.

The last thing that is significant about my childhood up to the age of eleven was that I was sexually abused as a child, let's just say by a stranger, as I ended up confronting this person when I was nineteen and getting to a level of forgiveness. But this repeated sexual abuse damaged me significantly although, I would bury the abuse deep in my mind until I started having flash backs at the age of nineteen with my boyfriend at University in the USA.

Only then would I come to understand the difficulties of overcoming sexual abuse and for other girls/boys or women who suffered rape, how damaging it is and this is something I wish men would understand. A United Nations Women's report, although statistics vary, states that between 35%-70% of girls/women worldwide have experienced sexual abuse and sexual violence. Furthermore, 200 million women and girls have undergone female genital mutilation in thirty countries most before the age of five. I find this beyond heinous and deplorable. But then, so much of the world I find difficult to understand like starvation, ISIL, paedophilia, sexual abuse and murder. Sometimes I find humanity extremely sick but then I think Ernst Hemingway had a point when he said, "Happiness in intelligent people is the rarest thing I know." I understand what he means by this because often is seems that people's happiness is based on their insensitivity, ignorant behaviours and indifference.

On my eleventh birthday in November 1986, my parents sat me down in the living room after my mother had found a packet of cigarettes in my horse-riding bag and told me that I would be going to a private co-ed boarding school starting in January 1987. I cried. I was a homebody and didn't want to be sent away to boarding school. During the next two years, I would experience my first bouts of depression that would sometimes have me lying in the school's sickbay for three days with non-stop crying. Thus, my teenage years would see the beginning of my journey with mild depression.

Chapter Two
Boarding School

I had just turned eleven before I started at my first boarding school, an Anglican private boarding school. I was nervous, shy and apprehensive about leaving home, however, two of my elder brothers were also going to boarding school in Brisbane as my parents spent more time in Sydney and overseas. I became very homesick over these years and was at times put in the school's sickbay for days at a time. I just could not stop crying. With hindsight I can look back on this as the beginning of my depression which would stay with me through my teenage years too.

I would play a lot of sport and make many friends during these years at this boarding school. A couple of these friends would stay in my life for years to come; however, as my mental health deteriorated in my 30s and I had the delusion that Illuminati Wizards would take control, I started to retreat from friendships and isolate.

I was at this boarding school for two years, and a year after I left, one of the boarding house masters would face justice. This boarding house master was a creep. I met him in my first term at boarding school and he seemed to take a fancy to me and make perverted comments.

I was made school prefect in my second year and he would invite me into his room in the morning before classes. I believe nothing happened between me and this boarding school master other than that he used to dress in front of me putting on his shirt and trousers. I realise in hindsight he was trying to groom me. He used to talk about wanting me to stay with him for the summer holidays and he thought if I stayed with him for eight weeks, I would get a suntan. On a school trip down to Canberra to play in Netball competitions, this boarding house master drove me back up to Sydney to my father's. He talked about his previous school he was at in NSW and the girls there. I guess I was highly suspicious of him. I did not know the word paedophile at that stage. I was twelve years old.

I believe I was lucky, however, after I left this boarding school, the next girl was not lucky and my silence and not speaking out meant that someone was abused. Decades later, after Social Services visited me in 2012 and stated in their report that my biggest risk factor is sexual exploitation, little did I know that it would become rampant in a way I could not even fathom, in the astral field. But I will get to that much later as that all involves my mental health as well.

A media report on this boarding house master was published in the newspaper and stated that he was found slumped in his car, gassed by its exhaust fumes. He also left a suicide note which the media reported that he revealed he had loved 20 girls at the school and at another school in Australia.

This boarding house master was reported to Police by a strong girl and how courageous of her. Sometimes I feel my silence about him meant girls were abused and for this I feel responsible and guilty even to this day.

I have no idea if I was mentioned in his suicide note; however, when I was at my next boarding school in Brisbane the Police called to speak with me. However, I was denied taking the call and talking to the Police as the school told me they did not want me involved or to be contacted by the Police.

The police have never contacted me again other than to arrest me or do welfare checks on me. You see a major theme throughout my life has felt like sexual exploitation.

The last thing I heard was that the boarding house master gassed himself to death in his car. I don't care, I'm glad he did. I hate paedophiles. Suffice to say, I am tired of my silence and the secrecy that has surrounded my life. Also, my silence means I have not protected others.

During my school holidays I would return to my parents; mainly they were living in Sydney then. We all went as a family on a holiday to Thailand and Bali and I remember this well as it was at Christmas time 1987 before my last year at this co-ed boarding school. The reason I remember this overseas trip itself is that I had my first period in Thailand near the Thai-Burma

Railway from World War II. I was so embarrassed and didn't really know what to expect with a period, so I used toilet paper the whole time instead of telling my mother and getting some pads. I was too shy to tell my parents. We also went to Hong Kong on another trip and I went on a business trip with my father and mother to Papua New Guinea although my parents left me in the hotel one night whilst they went out and that scared me. Suffice to say I was a nervous and worried child.

My teacher in Grade 6 at this co-ed boarding school was Mr Smith. He was a great teacher and knew that I struggled with my schoolwork and learning. To be honest I didn't have a clue why I had to learn all this stuff like math and spent most of my time daydreaming and staring out the window. He told me that I have my own 'special language' when I wrote and tried to help me with some private tutoring. To me, school and lessons were a waste of time and I just wanted to play sport, go swimming training, go on our school sailing trips and have fun.

In Year 7, I cannot remember the name of my teacher, but he had a nervous breakdown (or so we were told) and we mainly had substitute teachers. At one stage, he was crying in the classroom and I didn't understand why. I feared him. Fear is something that people experience towards those who have mental health problems; particularly like mine as they think you may be dangerous. But I would learn this much later in life.

One thing I do remember regarding my classes was that we would have to go to the library and watch the Iraq and Iran War on the news. 'Current events' I think the teachers used to call it. I found it strange, but more importantly, it made me anxious. In one way, I do not know why I mention this; part of my delusion I guess is that I thought militaries were somehow involved in my life. However, it would be decades later until I would have the severe delusion that I thought the militaries were all over my life and this was something to do with Australia wanting to become a Republic.

I recall that we had a visit from another boys' school to play sport and have dinner with them. I remember this because it was the first time, I was called fat by a boy and learnt of their judgement about my body which later in my life would get worse with men saying I had fat thighs and saggy breasts.

Our music teacher at this co-ed boarding school was fantastic; however, she too had an emotional breakdown over her husband and divorced; she told us he cheated on her. I was learning so much about relationships and their fragility. Nervous breakdowns by teachers, divorces, cheating husbands. I was twelve years old and learning a lot about life. Little did I know that in decades ahead I would learn so much about things I had not even imagined or thought possible.

At one stage in my last year, my father spoke to me and said that there is a girl from the USA that is coming to boarding school and that she is divorcing her father. I thought this was the strangest thing I had heard. How could you divorce a parent? But it is something that seemed to be able to happen in the USA. I cannot remember her name, but I showed her around school and hoped I helped her settle in.

One of my best memories is the camping trips we used to do. I loved them. There were also sailing weekend trips and I remember one, as it was the time, I had my first kiss, and the first time I got to sail on a catamaran, one of my most favourite types of sailing boats. I loved getting the catamaran up on its side and flying through the wind across the water. It was liberating and freeing, and I enjoyed the sense of danger of tipping over that it brought. Many times, it did, but I always got back up and sailed again. I had some great friends at school, and we were always changing best friends which is just something that we used to do, I guess. School friendships would get a lot harder for me once I went to my next boarding school and I would also suffer from homesickness and some mild depression.

Chapter Three
The Young Teenage Years

There are many things my dad taught me, one was, kill or be killed. Little did he know that would come into effect decades later. Not kill literally but stand up for yourself.

Before I delve into my years at my next private boarding school, there is a premise I wish to mention. For my teenage years, I went to all-girls boarding schools, schools where you are taught to be assertive, to be change agents in the world. To be change agents in our selected careers. To understand and advocate for justice. To challenge the status quo. To be women who are assertive and a voice in our communities, public and private organisations and in our world. To be active in our communities and politics and to challenge leaders. To not allow men to overpower you but to stand in your own empowerment. To have critical thinking and critical reasoning skills and to use them. To strive for excellence in all endeavours and work hard and play hard to achieve results, not just for ourselves but for others as well. They were not raising feminists. They were raising young girls, soon to be women, to be the best that they could be. Some of these women now, that I went to school with then, are leaders in their field; the media reports of them being rising stars and on the power lists. My journey, however, has been very different.

I mention this premise, what these girls' schools were like and are like because I would have delusions decades later that their raising of me would be challenged and put to the test in the most profound, unfathomable and heinous way by intelligence agencies and militaries.

In January 1989, I started Year 8 at this new boarding school in Brisbane, Australia. I was thirteen years old. I remember suffering from low levels of depression and still occasionally homesickness. Academically, I was not doing very well. I was struggling to study and to take my schoolwork seriously and it would be a while until I would hear the words, I think when I was once watching Oprah, "Education is your freedom."

I played a lot of sport, had at times, challenging friendships with girls, which I learnt later that that is something girls just do. One of my friends had epilepsy and one day had a seizure on the way to a basketball match. I had never had the experience of someone suffering epilepsy and so I went to the nearest store and asked them to call the ambulance. We did not have mobile phones in those days. I learnt about epilepsy after this and learnt how to care for someone who is having a seizure. Likewise, we had lifesaving training at school, part of the Royal Life Saving Society. Mainly, this was how to resuscitate someone who has drowned, and we all had exams to take at school to achieve these lifesaving qualifications.

It was also in this year that my parents would move to London, UK and I would remain in Australia in boarding school.

I joined the debating team at this boarding school where we would debate against other schools on current affairs or philosophical issues. I loved debating. I was always the first speaker laying out the position and argument of our team which would be challenged by the other debate team. I did not feel shy or nervous of this but felt in my element. I would stay in the debating team for three years and form skills in forming arguments, clarification of premises, providing well-constructed arguments back when challenged, confidence in talking to an audience and critical reasoning skills. These foundation skills that I learnt during these years I was in the debating team would be further developed in years to come.

In sometime in 1989 or 1990, my father would attend the Executive Program a Harvard University in the USA. I was immensely proud of my dad and his continued achievements since he left school at the age of 15, had never been to university and had worked his way up the corporate ladder. His admission to Harvard University was impressive to me and instigated my own desire to attend university overseas when the time came. However, I was torn on whether this would be in the UK or in the USA.

During this time, I would do more travelling with my parents to New York, Los Angeles, Hawaii and the UK.

When my mother took me and my brothers to Hawaii, I remember visiting the Pearl Harbor War Museum and learning about the USA's World War II involvement. It also provoked a sense of interest to me and I became fascinated by WWII history as my grandfather had served in WWII. My grandfather served for God, King, country and although I do not remember the date he enlisted in the infantry, the oath that he took was the Oath of Enlistment in the Australian Imperial Forces and as stated by the Australia War Memorial was, "I ... swear that I will well and truly serve our Sovereign Lord, the King, in the Military Forces of the Commonwealth of Australia until the cessation of the present time of war and twelve months thereafter or until sooner lawfully discharged, dismissed, or removed, and that I will resist His Majesty's enemies and cause His Majesty's peace to be kept and maintained, and that I will in all matters appertaining to my service faithfully discharge my duty according to law. So help me God."

In truth, I come from a long line of family members who have served in the military on my mother's side. My great-great grandfather served in the Boer War, my great grandfather in WWI at Gallipoli and my grandfather in WWII. It's kind of ironic that the word is Imperial Forces as this is a *Star Wars* phrase. However, I will explain that much later.

The reason that I mention this oath now is that when my mental health deteriorated and my Schizophrenia took hold later in my life, I had the severe delusion that the Australian Republican Movement would force me to enter a silent war over Australia becoming a Republic. Also, I believed in my delusion that some other countries would secretly support Australia and actively work towards making it a Republic. I did not understand this, however, until I was living at Emily's house in Sydney in 2012 where the USA Declaration of Independence was posted on her wall. I'm sure my psychiatrist would call this a delusion. What's so strange is that Australia cannot become a Republic unless they have a Referendum. I personally don't support Australia becoming a Republic nor would I vote for them too.

Nonetheless, I was always amazed that my grandfather survived the war with no PTSD or combat stress and went on to have a successful career and life although he did not talk to his daughter until my dad and mum married. He was estranged from my mum for the first twenty-one years of her life. I often wonder what that was like for my mum and what it was like growing up in the 1940's and 1950's as a child.

I recall the first time I went to the UK as it was winter, and we were flying in for landing at Heathrow Airport and I had just vomited in the airline vomit bag. I was staring out the window looking at the houses below so quaint and picturesque. It was grey and raining. Going to the UK felt colossal to me, and it was my first holiday there. The culture shock on me was significant, their British accent like music in my ears. But I felt out of depth, out of my league. A new world had opened for me on my first trip to the UK and in a way, strangely, I felt I had come home.

You see, when I as a child at my first State School I used to watch Princess Diana and Prince Charles's wedding movie, my own VHS video my parents bought me. It was not a VHS video just of their wedding (no we did not have DVDs in those days) but of how they met. I used to get up at 5am every Saturday and Sunday morning and watch this video, sitting on the carpet floor inches from the TV screen. I loved it. I loved their story and as a little girl I wanted to be a princess, like little girls do, like Princess Diana. I was only six years old. It was also the time that I would, like so many people in the world, fall in love with Princess Diana and I was one of them.

The reason I also mention Princess Diana and Prince Charles is because they visited Brisbane when I was at school there and we all lined up on Kingsford Smith Drive and waved as they drove by. One girl was lucky enough to hold out flowers for Princess Diana which made me rather jealous because I wanted to hold the flowers to give to her. I remember meticulously doing my hair that morning before going to school and having two pigtails on either side with beautiful satin brown ribbons tied onto them above the band. I was so excited to see Princess Diana and Prince Charles as I wanted to go home with them. Silly little thoughts I had as a child. So silly, but I was only about eight years old.

My first visit to the UK after my parents had moved there (I was thirteen years old), we stayed in a house in Wimbledon before they moved to another house around the corner from the

Wimbledon Tennis Courts. This was also my first introduction to Jane Austin novels which are literally the first books I read because I never bothered reading the books' they assigned us in English class at school. I fell in love with Jane Austin novels and there would begin my fantasy world that I could escape into and dream of the English gentleman. It also began my fascination with history in a country so stoked in history; I felt alive. I would also read other English authors and develop a concerned and serious interest in novels and true stories about World War II and the Holocaust and Auschwitz. I learnt the capability of the human species for utter cruelty. Finally, I developed an interest in reading after finding these novels and authors that I enjoyed so much.

My mother would take us up for trips to London and elsewhere, where we would visit Winston Churchill's War Rooms, Buckingham Palace, Oxford University, Cambridge University, Trafalgar Square, Shakespeare's birth town Stratford-upon-Avon, and countless castles. I was amazed, the history, the strength and power that I felt emanating and the intelligence that I had not ever come across before.

Over the next three years, until I was sixteen years old, I would travel to the UK twice a year for Christmas holidays and June/July holidays. By the age of fourteen, my parents introduced me to the West End theatres and musicals, Opera at the Royal Opera House and the Royal Ballet. I would sit then and soak up the wonder and talent and sophistication that I felt opened to. La Traviata, Aida, La bohème, Tristan and Isolde operas would be music to my ears, and I would buy the cassette tapes of these operas, so I could listen to them at home. My mother also took me and my brother to countless Shakespeare plays which were hard to understand at first and I would not fully be open to them until I started studying Shakespeare at a prestigious British girls' boarding school. Other things my parents took me to were, the Royal Enclosure at Ascot and the Wimbledon Tennis. My parents were active in soaking me up in the culture and wonder of Britain and I loved it. All of it.

I guess the only significant thing left about my days at my last boarding school in Brisbane in Australia was that in my last year there, Year 10, before I moved to the UK permanently, I had a boyfriend that my friend set me up with. His name was Steve and he was pointed out to me by my friend as someone for me to date. With my head stuck in Jane Austin novels, I had no idea why I had to date anyone. Boys were just not interesting to me. Regardless, at the age of fifteen I had my first boyfriend who would kiss me and tasted liked cheese and onion chips which I found entirely revolting. He went to a boys' boarding school in Brisbane and would come over sometimes in the afternoon and we would hide in the stairwells and kiss, me half suffocating on his cheese and onion chip breath. This was of course not allowed by my school, so I guess it was my first deviant act; meeting a boy afterschool which was not allowed.

I guess I mention Steve as I did introduce him to my parents and invited him to my 16th birthday party that my parents threw for me in Brisbane in September 1991. But my relationship with him also exposed me to the aggressiveness of boys and men and how much their sexuality dictates their existence. He wanted more from me than just kissing. But I only wanted to kiss. That's it. At the age of fifteen, reading Jane Austin and dreaming of a British gentleman there was no way I would do more than kiss. Little did I know I would grow into a woman one day and my sexuality would begin to shock me. However, not at that age.

I was very attached to my morals and values as a teenager. You see, I wanted to save myself for a husband because I believed throughout my teenage years to remain a virgin and honour a man, a husband on my wedding night. I was quiet attached to these values as a teenager, and whilst I was a teenager, nobody was going to get in the way of that. So, I said no to Steve and that we could only kiss. His response was that he went and had sex with another girl who had very large breasts, which he told me about, and that it was great. I thought, *Good, someone wants to have sex with you, it will not be me.* It would not be the last time Steve would bug me for sex. Two more times he did when I was at my own 16th birthday party and at a party I went to at Noosa. But I just said no. We broke up then.

In December 1991, I left Australia and flew to the UK. A new door was opening for me at a prestigious British girls' boarding school. I had miraculously passed the entrance exam and I would start in January 1992. I would have to repeat a year as I had missed the first term and, in hindsight, I could have left Australia a lot earlier to go to school in the UK as my brother had already been accepted into a prestigious British Boys' Boarding School and was in attendance there.

I guess I want to say that I have had anxiety since I was a child, which at times can make me feel quite frightened, and I can honestly say there are only two times I have felt entirely safe in my life with no anxiety. The first, being when I attended this prestigious British Girls' Boarding School from 1992-1994 and the second time, when I had my first admission to a mental health hospital in the UK; in Surrey in February 2013.

Chapter Four
England

For Christmas in 1991, when I was sixteen, my father asked me what I wanted as a present. I asked for a gold cross with Jesus Christ on it. Well, literally Jesus nailed to the cross, his crucifixion. A reminder to me, of what humanity does to Archangels and the Son of God. This gold cross with Jesus Christ on it, intricately engraved with his crucifixion, was very important to me. Somehow it felt like it gave me protection. Also, I was soon to find out that many girls at my future school would wear them.

That Christmas, I would get all the supplies from my new British Girls' Boarding School to start mid-year in January 1992 in Lower Sixth Form. Upon reflection, I sometimes think back to my time at this School as something out of a Harry Potter book. Not literally with magic and wands but with the old school trunks we had to pack all our cloths in, the navy-blue long cloaks and the school dining room where we would take our meals. I would often wear that long blue cloak whilst riding on my bike to classes in those cold and raining winters.

In the second week of January, my parents drove me to this prestigious British Girls' Boarding School where a new adventure awaited me. I was nervous, still in culture shock and very worried about my academics. You see, in Australia and for the last ten years of my education I paid no attention in classes. In fact, I didn't even see the point in why I had to go to school and learn all these subjects like biology and chemistry neither of which I cared for. I had limited interest in History in Australia as it was focused on local history and I wanted to learn about world history. I had no interest in English class as I didn't like the novels, they asked me to read so I never read them. Art was about the only subject I was interested in which I achieved a B grade in. This would all change at this British School.

As I entered school mid-year, I would have to repeat the Lower Sixth Form, as advised by the school, so I choose subjects that I would not be doing when I started my A Levels. So, I choose Classics and Art History. I failed at the end of the term; however, it gave me the opportunity to see the standard and level of studying needed to succeed at Oxbridge A Levels. Once I started my A Levels in September 1992, I chose History, English Literature and Economics and Maths A/S. I have no idea why I choice Maths since I hated it and eventually dropped it as an A Level.

I felt like I was in a new world. I was taught and tutored by the best and brightest. Teachers from Cambridge University, Oxford University and University College London. I was mesmerised by their level of intelligence and loved the subjects I was taking, particularly History which included the Tudor period and thereafter, and WWII history including the period of the Russian Revolution and Stalin. I also learnt about the French Revolution and the fall of the aristocracy in France. Most of all, I studied WWII, that started with the invasion of Poland, and the Nazi Regime. I was in my element. I had found at school, for once in my life, subject content that I was fascinated in, and so I studied. I studied very hard.

I made very good friends at this British School and many of these women are in the world today as leaders and influences in their selected professions. They taught me to study hard and would often take me to the library where we would be studying endlessly until late in the evening. Many of them went on to Cambridge University and Oxford University. It was amazing to be surrounded by young women of such intelligence as they influenced me and helped me to be the best that I could be.

During my holidays, my parents would take me to Europe where I would saturate and indulge myself in its history, its glorious architecture, museums and cultures. Europe fascinated me as it was so diverse, each country speaking its own language, having its own culture and managing to work together as the European Union. In Paris, I would wonder the streets with my family tasting the delicacy of Nutella crepes bought from street vendors as we would explore the sites, churches and museums.

The Louvre Museum exploded in me a love of art and the opportunity to see its most prized possession, the *Mona Lisa*. The passion of the French language on my ears reminded me of the remnants of my French lessons at school in Australia, where I desperately tried to learn European languages but was frankly not a linguist. My parents would take me many more times to Paris, and I enjoyed each trip.

During the Easter holidays from school, my parents would take me skiing in Austria with my brother. I had skied before, as my parents had taken me to the ski slopes since I was four years old in Australia. On one ski trip, I met an Australian ski instructor, Charles, who was teaching in Austria at the time and he invited me out for drinks with his friends. He was thirty-two years old and I was sixteen. Needless to say, I could not hold my alcohol and vomited everywhere in the bathroom and all through my hair.

After the first summer from my Lower Sixth year, before I started in Lower Sixth again and began my A Levels, my parents rented a house in Tuscany, Italy for the holidays. There I would soak up the Italian culture and explore cities like Florence and Sienna. It reminded me of the movie *Room with a View* and the romanticism of Italy would be something that stayed with me throughout my life. Further holidays in Italy would take me to Rome and seeing Da Vinci's Sistine Chapel where I would marvel at the talents of humanity past.

In September 1992, I would start my A Levels with the girls who had just finished their GCSEs. I made new friends in this year and lived one of the boarding houses with them. I was nervous to have to make friends again, however, I soon learnt to adjust but more importantly focus on my studies. Located up in the main school was the Lower Sixth Form study room where we would share a room with one other student for study time or for breaks between classes. We would also listen to music, my dad had bought me a music stereo, and we would play Queen and Red Hot Chilli Peppers. Most of all, I loved studying and loved my subjects. Economics taught me all about micro- and macro-economics and the European Union. History would teach me all about the 20th century and the Tudor Period. Moreover, I would begin to learn to write essays, read endlessly and form better and more advanced critical thinking skills.

A friend of mine in the year above helped me further by providing me with a student tutor at Oxford University where I went for the weekend and spent two days being tutored in History and essay writing. This markedly improved my writing skills and the ability to structure arguments. My weekend at Oxford University was amazing and I would go many times to meet my friends who were studying there. It would also instigate my interest in wanting to apply to Oxford University, something I would do in my following year.

In Christmas 1992, one of my friends from Brisbane, Australia would come over to England to visit me and this British School I was attending. However, I suffered from some homesickness and was crying for two days. I do not remember feeling depressed, however, it's important to note that during my teenage years I did have some depression, but I never had any delusions, hallucinations or heard any voices.

Towards the end of my Lower Sixth year, the Lower Sixth and Upper Sixth had to vote, along with the teachers, on who was to be Head of School and School Captain (deputy). This ended up being my first introduction to a little politics. I must make the point clear here that many girls, most even, had been at this British School for six years. I had only been there for eighteen months. The next morning, after the voting had taken place, I was asked to see my boarding house mistress. I went to her study early and she told me that the Headmistress would like to see me. She didn't seem too impressed. So, I jumped on my bike and went to the Headmistress' house. There she sat me down and told me that I would be the next Head of School. I was astounded. I questioned her and said what about another girl as she has been here longer than me and my year may have a problem with it. But the Headmistress reassured me, and I accepted the position. I had become the new Head of School after only eighteen months there. I felt immensely proud and very honoured.

Chapter Five

Present Day Psychosis

It's the 19th of April 2018 today. My son's birthday. I have not felt much like writing in the last week and this afternoon I sit on the grass in the park watching the autumn leaves fall, dripping their amber and red colours across the lawn. My motivation is low. All that keeps spinning around in my head is that there will not be any justice for all that they did. This depresses me. I am rambling and muttering to myself.

I keep being told through the brain chip and body possessions, there will never be any justice. Voices saying, "Stop writing, dink, bitch." My motivation is zapped.

To all intents and purposes, I cannot write my psychosis right now. It would be considered too defamatory but also since my delusions are so active at the moment, I'm not going into them. But I write them in my notepad. My goal is recovery, stability and a wonderful life.

I will say that in my delusions, I feel my human rights have been violated by intelligence agencies, militaries and political leaders. That's as much as I can explain right now.

I still have the serious desire, but what I call a delusion, that I get to sit before the United States Congress, a Congressional Hearing, and make a statement to them. But I cannot write and explain that to you either.

I am in chronic psychosis. That's what they tell me.

Alas, this is what the psychiatrists call delusions and that nothing happened. These are my thoughts, but I am moving too far ahead, and it may not make much sense. So back to the British School days.

Chapter Six
Head of School

I called my parents when it was announced at assembly that I was Head of School. I was elated as were they. To be Head of School seemed like a dream come true, particularly, as I was Australian and not British. However, what this did introduce me to is the nature of a little politics. Some of the girls in my year were not very happy that I had been elected Head of School and thus put together a petition to have me removed. I only found this out by my study roommate, and I was a little surprised, however, it did not eventuate into anything and I remained Head of School. I was also awarded Swimming Captain too.

My last year at this British School was mainly filled with studying for my final A Level exams. During this year, the Headmistress, along with my father, would introduce me to USA universities. The Headmistress suggested I apply to a USA University, in Washington DC, so I also sat my SATs in London. My SAT results were not great, I cannot remember what they were; however, I still applied to USA Universities and along with Oxford University and Edinburgh University to read Law.

Unfortunately, my boarding house mistress did not allow me to apply to St Edmunds College at Oxford and I had to apply to St Catherine's College. I was called for interview by Oxford in the winter of 1993 to sit an interview. I remember this clearly as one of the interview questions I could not answer. Suffice to say, I did not get into Oxford nor did I obtain the A Level grades required getting one A and two Bs.

For the USA universities, I had to write an essay which I did and applied to a University in Washington DC and went to an interview with at a University in Georgia. In January 1994, I was accepted into this University in Washington DC. I was excited, I was going to go to the USA to live and study and it seemed like a whole new world was opening up to me.

As the school year drew to an end, I auditioned for the school musical which was an adaptation of Noel Coward and Cole Porter. I had to sing a song in front of an audience of school and parents including my own. I was very nervous, but it was a pleasure to do.

I had to write and give a speech for School Speech Day (graduation) and I read a few speeches in order to prepare for it. To this day, I cannot remember much of what I wrote nor the speech that I gave, however, I stood in front of all the students and parents and gave this speech not feeling anxious or shy. I was eighteen years old, accepted into this University in what could be called the most powerful city in the world, Washington DC. Little did I know that this next chapter of my life would expose me to the drug world. I had spent my teenage years opposed to drugs and adamant that I would never touch or take them.

After graduation, four other girls and I decided to go backpacking through Europe and here I felt the first sense of my freedom. Five girls back packing though France, Germany, Austria, Italy, Czechoslovakia and Greece. I had been to Europe many times with my parents but not by myself with friends. It was an incredible experience and lasted a month. We met many different people who were also backpacking and in Czechoslovakia, we met two American men who were from the US and one who was also at university in Washington DC. I cannot remember his name, but we spent the night together wondering the streets of Prague till the early hours of the morning, talking, drinking beer and discussing how I was moving to Washington DC in August 1994. We kissed. We kissed a lot and he wanted more than that, but I said no. We stayed in contact as he gave me his number and I caught up with him in Atlanta, Georgia before I went to University.

In August 1994, I flew over to Atlanta, Georgia, with my parents to the flat they had there as my father had been working in Atlanta quite a bit. I called the American guy I had met in Prague and went to a Lollapalooza music festival with him and his friends. It was the first live concert and music festival I had ever been to and the freedom I felt after being in boarding schools for eight years was magnificent. However, I remember him driving me home and asking me for sex on the back seat of his car. I said no, and he walked me up the stairs to my parents flat. He would try and contact me again once I was in Washington DC, however, I would not ever see him again.

During these weeks in Atlanta before I started my freshman year at University, my parents would arrange for me to meet a man who was already at this University called Jack. My parents arranged for him to take me out to dinner and discuss this University and what it's like along with providing a contact at University for me. Little did I know that I would fall for this man quickly and rather desperately once I started my freshman year.

Jack came and picked me up and took me out to dinner to a restaurant called Houston's where we ordered spinach dip and chicken with black beans, I think. I felt quite a bit of culture shock and this was only the second time in my life I had spoken to an American guy. I was very nervous. American men are different, you see. Well to me, they are. So confident, so easily do they speak and make conversation. He smoked Camel cigarettes and offered me one in his car. I was so incredibly nervous. My parents told me he was Jewish as many of my parents' friends were Jewish in Atlanta.

Nonetheless, Jack made me feel comfortable and I enjoyed my dinner with him. I would soon see him at University in Washington DC and my world would change in many ways.

A couple of days before my mother was due to drive me up to Washington DC and help me move into my new University dorm, I was taken to a Liza Minnelli concert in Atlanta with some friends of theirs. Little did I understand that Liza Minnelli's mother would come through in spirit in 2017.

The reason I remember this concert and mention it is that the wife of my father's friend said to me, "You will be ruined at University in the USA." There I am in my long navy-blue dress with my Jesus Christ crucifixion necklace being told I am going to be ruined. I did not understand this but, in a way, she was telling the truth. Not that I blame others, as so much of my four years at University in Washington DC were about choices I made, and I must be accountable and responsible for my choices.

Around the 20th August 1994, my mother drove me the ten-hour trip up to Washington DC. We arrived at the University car park where we were met by students helping us freshman move into our dorm rooms. I was eighteen years old and going to University in the USA, and I was shy and nervous. Little did I know that it would also expose me to the drug world.

Chapter Seven
University in Washington DC

Walking up the stairs to my new dormitory, I felt excited to finally be going to university. My parents did not get the opportunity to attend university although my father, as an adult, went to Harvard University for three months when I was a teenager. I didn't really get much choice on what I wanted to study. I had applied to the School of Business although at times in my life I wish I had studied History or Law, but I think, I did not encourage myself to study those subjects, in particular History, as I felt it would not lead to much of a career later.

As the students lead me to my dorm room, I met my roommate called Becky. I was a little shocked at the size of the rooms. There was a bunk bed, cupboard, desk and an en-suite bathroom. Having had my own room for the last year at my British School, it felt a little cramped to be bunking with someone again. I cannot really say that Becky and I got along that well. I'm not sure she wanted to room with a foreigner for that matter, but I took it in my stride and settled in and started to meet other people on my floor.

I was shocked when I went around the corner of the dorm to find that the men were also rooming on the same floor as the girls. This shocked me, not surprisingly, as I had gone to all-girls schools since I was thirteen. I had no idea how to relate to men. I had no idea how to relate to American men who were so confident, chatty and what seemed to me, rather cool. I would listen to the American guys on my floor talk in their thick American accent which excited me and intimidated me at the same time. They had gone to co-ed high schools and were used to girls being around. To me, it was all a bit of a culture shock. But more than that, to be honest, their accent sexually aroused me, and this was confusing to me and made me nervous. It was not something that I had come across, nor ever felt before.

I must be honest here as this is when I started smoking cigarettes. I had smoked a few cigarettes with my friends in Europe but now I went and bought a packet of Camel cigarettes and started smoking outside the dormitory with some of the other guys and girls. In a way, it was an icebreaker as it helped me to meet people.

In my first week at University in Washington DC, Jack, who was in junior year, came over to my dormitory to see how I had settled in and gave me a six-pack of beer. He invited me to his house that night which he and three fellow friends lived at. It was my first party that I had been invited too. However, it was the first time in my life I had come into contact with drugs that night. Marijuana. I had been totally against drugs and that night I was offered bong hits of marijuana. In an effort to fit in, I accepted. I smoked pot. Drank beer and laughed along with everyone at the party. This was the first step in betraying my values and set me on a path that would lead to a drug and alcohol rehabilitation centre four years later.

I became close friends with some of the guys on my dorm floor namely Pete and Ralph. During this time, I was seeing Jack frequently and Ralph took me out for coffee and talked to me about sticking to my values and not having sex until I was married. He was Catholic, and we often had theological discussions. I liked how Ralph cared about me and he knew that Jack was a junior and that I wanted to save myself for marriage. These are the ideals and values that formed strongly in my teenage years and I did not want to let them go. But I would. I decided to.

My friend Pete, a freshman from my dormitory floor, was campaigning for the Student Council, I think, if I remember correctly. One afternoon, we were outside on the terrace and he asked me to come over with him to another residence hall to meet some ROTC sophomores. ROTC stands for Reserved Officers' Training Corps, future students who would serve in the US Armed Forces after graduating from university. Pete probably does not even remember but I was too shy to go and meet them. Little did I know I would meet them three years later.

The impact of drinking beer and smoking pot with friends, which started to become a regular thing, would drastically change my life path. Some of my freshman male friends from my dormitory grew concerned over my hanging out with Jack all the time and also the appearance that we would end up dating. One afternoon whilst I was at Jack's, he introduced me to a close friend of his called Sue. After meeting her and chatting, I, later that night, confronted Jack and said that he should date Sue as they seemed so close. He said 'no' to me, that he had tried to date her his freshman year, but it didn't work out. I pressed him again as my intuition was screaming at me that they were to be together. He said 'no.' But I was right about their connection as after University they would be together, marry and have a family. I only wish I had declined his advances on me and trust my intuition about him and Sue. Years later in my life, some would call me clairvoyant. But I don't think I am.

On September 13th, 1994 when I was eighteen years old, stoned from pot and drunk from beer at 3am in the morning, I asked Jack to have sex with me and thus began my three-year relationship with him. At times I felt that Jack was a wonderful and caring man, but I felt lost at University in Washington DC and I'm not sure my intentions were in my best interests. However, I enjoyed many of my years at University with him.

Jack was pre-med and wanted to be a surgeon when I meet him. However, over the duration of our relationship, he would move away from this goal to in future, run the family business. I fell in love with Jack and it was my first relationship. But my partying, and not studying, would affect my grades.

Chapter Eight
The ROTC Guys

I do not wish to carry on too much about my relationship with Jack. I reflect on it now that I was stoned a lot and I do not think, whilst doing drugs along with LSD a couple of times, really provided me with any sound mind to make healthy choices. But I was inseparable from him, but it felt like more co-dependence than anything. However, he treated me very well and we enjoyed many Dave Matthews concerts together and I became a bit of a Dave Matthews Band groupie. Once, at a concert in Virginia, I met Dave Matthews backstage and found their music awesome.

I guess there is just a few things left to mention about my relationship with Jack which ended abruptly in my junior year after I met Simon. Whilst I was with Jack, I had flashbacks to childhood sexual abuse which came back as memories in November 1994.

I remember lying on Jack's s bedroom floor sobbing and anxious as flashback after flashback would come through my mind. I told him. He was so kind about it all and arranged and paid for therapy for me and for that I am eternally grateful to him. He was so kind and generous to me back then. I mention this because it is the first time, I would come into contact with the mental health system and therapy. During this time, I saw my first psychiatrist who diagnosed me, I think, with depression. However, I cannot remember if I was prescribed any anti-depressants. Needless to say, I did a year in therapy to overcome the trauma and get on with life. Thank you, Jack, for helping me.

I mention the drugs I took at University in Washington DC because psychiatrists see them as one of the environmental triggers for Schizophrenia although at University, I don't recall having any Schizophrenia symptoms.

In my third year at University, junior year, Jack had graduated, and I was living with friends in a house on P Street in Washington DC. It is during this year that my drinking became a problem. I turned 21 years old and was now legally able to drink and thus would be at the University bar occasionally, along with down at the M Street bars in Washington DC. After living with Jack for two years, I was alone now and the long-distance relationship with him was hard for me.

I had a large 21st birthday party which my parents arranged, and my brothers came to from overseas. I had put on quite a bit of weight by then from all the drinking and eating. That was probably the last time Jack and I were ever really getting along and thereafter our relationship would deteriorate, and he and Sue would get together. But not before I met Simon, an ROTC man who I fell for hard and fast and thought to myself, with him, this is what love really feels like. But I am getting ahead of myself here.

Sometime at the end of 1996, I would have my first drinking charge from the Police. I was drinking at a bar on M Street with a few friends, one of whom was not yet 21 years old. I cannot remember what the charge was, but I was handcuffed and put into a police cell. To me, this was a message that my life was completely off the rails and my drinking was a problem. Moreover, I would become known to the University Drug and Alcohol Student Affairs team and had to attend drug and alcohol counselling. However, I did not stop drinking.

In the last semester of my junior year, Pete, my former dorm room friend, came to see me and asked if I would be a date for someone at a US Military Ball in Washington DC. I was to go as Stuart's date along with others including Pete and the ROTC guys who were graduating namely Simon and Paul. I told him yes but, I would need to get a dress.

I took myself to Sacks Fifth Avenue in Bethesda and bought a silk cream-coloured dress with very thin straps on the back. It was not a dress you could wear a bra with so that afternoon, before the US Military ball I showered, shaved my legs and slipped on the dress and cream high-heeled shoes. It was the first ball I had been asked too. The first, and my last, US Military Ball I would ever be asked too. But I was excited and nervous. The thing is though, I cannot remember a thing about it, and this baffles me a lot.

I cannot tell you how or with whom I arrived at the Ball with. I cannot tell you anything about it as the only memory I have is leaving the US Military Ball in bare feet, carrying my shoes and walking beside Stuart, Simon and Paul. Perhaps, I was just really drunk and in a three-hour blackout. Although I doubt it.

As I was walking in bare feet next to these ROTC Seniors of whom were all looking dashing and hot in their uniforms, Stuart would turn to me and tell me that he really likes me, has slept with many girls and he would like to have sex with me. I felt largely repulsed by the offer not least being told how many girls he had slept with. Suffice to say, we all went back to Simon and Paul's house in Washington DC to continue partying, and that is when I meet Simon that I can remember. Often during my life, I had wanted to ask Simon and Paul what happened at the Ball and why I took my shoes off? Perhaps they don't remember either. All I remember is coming to, walking down the street with them all trying to get taxis.

Back at Simon and Paul's house in the basement, the music went on and the dancing began. I had never seen guys so confident and dancing away to great tunes. No men I had been around had done this. It was there I think I told Simon and Paul what Stuart had said to me and I told them I didn't want to sleep with him. The next thing I know they are all wrestling and Stuart's leg gets broken and the ambulance came to take him to hospital. I will always be thankful to Simon and Paul for protecting me that night. It felt chivalrous and gentlemanly of them.

Simon was going into the US Army and Paul into the US Marines. Little did I know that in the future, I would have severe delusions that Simon and others would have to protect me from what I thought was astral projections from ISIS terrorists. But I'll get to explaining that later.

After the ambulance left, Simon took me to his room to go to sleep on his futon. He was a gentleman and he made no moves on me. He gave me a one of his immaculately ironed t-shirts to slip into. As I took off my dress, he politely turned away so as not to see me naked. He looked so handsome to me, his body divine and his energy magnetic. I loved everything about him,

47

his eyes, his nose, the thick American accent, his stature. They say falling in love with someone at first sight is the worst kind of love as it doesn't last. But for me, falling for him that night lasted for some time, although I know now it was lust and not love.

Chapter Nine
Simon

Today is May 20th, 2018. I have been in a manic-depressive episode for about three weeks now and all I can do is write through it and attend my therapy sessions. The suicidal ideation covets me like a thick blanket. Thoughts race through my mind wanting to end my life and these episodes of depression and Schizophrenia are too much to live with. My mental health care social worker tells me to think objectively and tell myself I am just going through a depressive episode and to use behavioural tactics to manage and CBT. I feel no one will ever read this book as I am not a writer. I feel I am crap at writing really. No one will believe my story and that there will not be any justice for those involved are above the law. These thoughts depress me more. But, still somehow, I want to try to write. The Zyprexa medication makes me feel a little docile. All I have now is my memory to work off. So, back to my University days of 1997 and Simon who I fell in love with.

Simon and I awoke the next morning and went up to the hospital to see Stuart. His leg was badly broken, and it was a few weeks until his graduation. If only I could remember the Military Ball, but I cannot. But I do remember dancing in Simon and Paul's basement and would have many more nights of dancing and drinking with them. It becomes a little blurry to me now, but I ended up going over to Simon's again, I think a night or two later, and drinking and dancing. It was the first time I met ROTC gentlemen and they would rock it up on the basement floor to music and dance away. I had so much fun with them but, more significantly, I felt desperately attracted to Simon. Late that night, he invited me upstairs and both of us being sweaty; he took me into the bathroom and started the shower. He kissed me, and we began to undress, the site of his body burned passion, lust and eroticism through my veins. That shower that night with him standing naked and feeling his skin against mine as the warm water splashed over my body was the most passionate experience I had had in my life. I moved my hand down to touch his manhood and tried to slide him between my legs. I wanted to make love to him so badly and to me, he radiated love and light, drinking in his energy, his strength, his power. I thought to myself, why did I not go and meet him in my freshman year when I had the opportunity?

Simon pulled away from me in the shower, turning off the taps as he said, "Come to my room." He handed me a towel and I dried myself whilst he did too, reaching out for his hand to hold as I followed him to his room. I will have to be honest with you here that I do not think that Simon felt the same way about me as I did for him. He was a senior, graduating in weeks and focused on having fun before entering into the US Army for his four years of service. Sometimes in life, I came to realise later in my life, people come into your life for a reason, a season or a lifetime. To me, Simon came into my life for a reason and a season, but in a way, his impact on me would stay with me for some of my lifetime.

We stood naked against each other in his room, kissing and gently touching the sensitive parts of our bodies. He lay me down on the futon, whilst he reached for a condom. That's something Simon always was good about, using protection. I don't know why I mention that as it makes it sound less passionate, but it also showed me Simon's responsible side. He lay down on top of me as I enveloped him and wrapped my legs around him, trembling, to take him in, so we felt like one. Afterwards we chatted and fell asleep. I felt I was in heaven.

I have to say at this point, when I met Simon, I was still dating Jack and as such, I had just cheated on him. It's the only time in my life that I cheated on a man, but it happened. I own that and take responsibility for it. Nothing would have stopped me being with Simon and for the weeks that lay ahead for both of us.

Simon and I would meet, sometimes at the Bar in Washington DC, other times at his house. My moments and experience of intimacy and sex with him would increase my desire, passion and lust for him. One afternoon, as the summer sun glistened through the afternoon sky, reflecting a glow in his room, we had sex on his bed. I was on top of him and totally taken in with his aura and energy; I just wanted to merge my spirit with his. As I sat and moved on top of him, my body reached peaks of pleasure resulting in my tenderness wetting him everywhere, including all over the sheets and into the mattress below. After he came, he reached his hand down besides his hip and felt the sheets below, saturated, wet with my desire of him. This had not happened to me before, and I was shocked. He said to me, "The sheets and mattress are wet." I felt so embarrassed. Totally embarrassed. Simon was a gentleman about it though. In a way, at the time, Simon didn't understand the impact he had on me mentally, physically and spiritually. He hopped up and changed the sheets, after which, we lay down together, embracing in the glorious sun spread-eagled over Washington DC that Sunday afternoon. I was so happy that day, that afternoon.

Simon used to call me 'cool cat'. Words that I would later, in my life, use along with Austin Powers, to signal him when I thought that I was in trouble or danger because I had delusions and I thought he was an intelligence agent. One afternoon, as we lay together on the futon sweaty from our sex, we talked, and he unveiled more about himself to me, his views, his thoughts, his goals and his family. Americans are very patriotic, and Simon is no exception as I would learn how patriotic he was and his love for his country. I find Americans patriotism so different from Australians, like when the United States national anthem plays, they stand and place their hand over their heart. I never experienced such honour in Australia and often Australians will not even stand when the national anthem is played. Many Australians may disagree with me on this, but it's been my experience.

Moreover, Simon explained to me that afternoon that he would have to do four years' service in the US Army after he graduated and that he then wanted to be a spy, like Austin Powers. He also talked of wanting to be an actor. If Simon really is a spy now, he possibly would get into a lot of trouble for that, telling me I mean, as all applications are meant to be secret. But at the time it was just a goal, and I felt intrigued that he would share that with me. More importantly, however, the way Simon talked about helping people, the environment, helping his mother, showed me his altruism, or altruistic side. During these chats, he talked to me about his name, but I cannot remember what he said. But, my response to him was something about a Presidents name like Truman. His aura was like that. We were both 21 years old then and I can honestly say he was totally altruistic and concerned for the welfare of others. He would change I know, once enlisted in the US Army, but I knew him before that, and he seemed sweet and divine.

Simon and I were complete opposites really. He was disciplined, confident, who cared about the environment, his diet, people. I was shy, reserved, smoking cigarettes, not giving a toss about exercise or my body. We seriously were opposites and to this day still would be. But, that's just one more thing that intrigued me more about him, as he was totally different to me and any man I had met before.

During these last few weeks at University before he graduated, I told him about Jack, and we discussed how I would need to fly down to Atlanta and break up with him. So that is what I did, and I explained to Jack that I had met someone else. I remember meeting Simon at a bar that night I got back with one of his roommates who was going into the US Air Force. My relationship with Jack ended that weekend, and within weeks, Jack would begin dating Sue and eventually marry her and have a family.

Simon would never understand, even though I talked to him about Australia, some Australians so-called desire to be a Republic, well some of them I should say. Decades later in my life, and with my delusions, I felt like this fight over Australia becoming a Republic would surround me and my children even though I would not know why. Often, in 2009 and 2010, I would scream in my head for Simon to help me and my children when I deluded myself that war games were going on with Australia trying to become a Republic, that people told me a drug cartel was around us and that I was being stalked by a business tycoon. In my severe delusion that Simon was a spy, I thought he could help. But I'll come to that later.

Sometimes you find in life, when you're walking on the clouds in a delusion of love, that things are too good to be true. I am not sure if it's true, but I think Simon possibly thought I had a problem with alcohol. I know he did once I was in my senior year and he was in the military. Simon would talk to me a week before his graduation and tell me that Paul's cousin was coming to his graduation and I had to go away and not be present. Also, his parents were coming. I was so shocked at this as I had just broken up with Jack and he never mentioned this other girl. Nonetheless, we had one final night together before his graduation where Simon took me to a classical orchestra concert in Washington DC which I thoroughly enjoyed. He seemed a gentleman and although I fell for him in more ways than I can imagine, our short relationship would come to an end.

One night, after I tried to go by his house to see him, Paul came out and talked to me on the street and said something along the lines that Simon does not want to be with you. I turned red with rage. I was so angry and, I had been drinking. So, I thought, *Screw you, Simon,* and I went and got my car, drink driving, and drove it all the way up into the University campus, right through the graduation chairs that were all setup. I was arrested that night, my second arrest at University which would lead me to the Drug and Alcohol Counsellors at Student Affairs. I did not see Simon's graduation and I did not hear from him again until I started my senior year at University.

Chapter Ten

My Beginnings with Alcoholics Anonymous

That summer, the summer of 1997, I stayed at University and in Washington DC until the end of June and really got up to no good. I was so angry that Simon had cut our connection and I went on a drinking, partying and having one-night stands rampage. I was not living my values that I held so dear in my teenage years. Anyway, that's what I call in now days. Thinking somehow, I could sleep my way out of feeling how I felt about Simon by being with other men. But it was no good. It simply made me feel ashamed and sad.

At the end of June, I flew back to London to stay with my parents and to do an internship at a consulting company. Part of my arrangement with the Drug and Alcohol Services at University was that I attend Alcoholics Anonymous (AA) meetings and see a Councillor in my senior year. However, I would not start attending AA meetings until I returned to Washington DC in September. There was a part of me that didn't want to return to Washington DC again. I felt I was trapped in a hole living there. I must also mention here that this was also the beginning of me wanting to isolate from friends. I ended up getting my own flat in my senior year and not stay in a house with friends like everyone else was doing. This isolationism was something that has significantly impacted my life and made my depression worse. Thus, in my senior year, I started to experience the beginnings of anxiety and depression which my sobriety made even more intense.

I started to feel shyer in my senior year. I was sober and attending AA meetings in Washington DC and living alone. I put my head down and studied to improve my grades which had been suffering. Moreover, I re-connected with Simon a couple of times down on the Military Base he was on in Georgia. It seemed, Simon would talk to me and re-kindle things now that I was sober. Well, this is what I thought anyway.

I drove down to the Military Base in Georgia a few times to see Simon. The most significant of that is the week I spent down there on fall break. I was sober, nervous to see him again and I felt intensely shy. If I can remember correctly, he had just tried to complete Green Beret or Ranger training but had broken his leg and thus, not completed the training. We talked about it a little and he mentioned that he wanted to try again. He also talked to me about his parachute training and that he would be moving to Texas. I learnt about his new life now in the military, he had changed already.

Simon had changed. But still secretly he kissed me in his uniform out on the balcony which he was not allowed to do in uniform.

Although he went to work during the day, and I studied, at night we would be together, and he took me to a cabin for the weekend with another couple. On the last weekend I was there, we went, with another soldier (a friend of his), to a place where games were played. I forget the name of it. It was here that Simon's friend took me aside and said to me to leave Simon alone, he does not want to be with you and go and live in New York. To this day, I will never know if Simon asked him to say those things or if his friend said it himself. Needless to say, I was shocked as these words did not match Simon's behaviour towards me and it seemed like a carrot and stick mentality. I always wondered if that carrot and stick mentality was Simon's.

I went to Georgia one more time to see Simon as I needed to change the number plates on my car. He met me at the hotel I was staying at and I pleasured him, but we did not have sex, nor did he pleasure me in return. I felt rather used and started to see that I was nothing more than a sexual object, something that would be reflected and occur throughout my life. Well that was my perception anyway. It would take me years to realise there's give and take in relationships.

My senior year at University was a sober year until my graduation week. My grades improved; I went to AA meetings. I saw Simon one more time in Washington DC whilst I was driving with my dear friend Anne who I spent a lot of time with. We talked and basically said goodbye to each other. He did not even let me know he was coming up to Washington DC for the weekend. In my reality, I never understood Simon, and to this day, I do not understand him.

It was during my senior year that I got wind of intelligence agencies. I am not saying that I had delusions about them then; however, I had a friend in one of my classes who talked about wanting to be an intelligence agent, wanting to be a spy. Her mentioning that in class triggered me, and for some reason I started to feel afraid. I don't know why intelligence agencies terrify me so much.

I think it was during my graduation week, I also met three men at a bar in Washington DC who introduced themselves to me and told me they were Secret Service men. I have no idea if that was a lie, it probably was a lie. They were on a bachelor party and they tried to set me up with the groom to be. I joined their table and drank beer with them and had loads of fun. They seemed to want me to hook up with the future groom. I politely declined and put him in a cab.

Alas, disaster had struck my graduation week. I fell of the wagon as they say. I was envious and jealous that my friends could drink, and party and I was sober. So, I started drinking. On the Wednesday night before graduation, which was on the Saturday, we were partying in a marquee in the parking lot behind the dormitories. A fellow friend of mine suggested we take one of golf carts that were outside the marquee and drive them to an off-campus party. I sat in the passenger seat and off we drove in this golf cart down the streets of Washington DC arriving at the party. It was not long after this occurred that the police arrived, and I was arrested for theft (of the golf cart). My friend, Zac, had vanished and never got in trouble for it even though he was the driver and it was his idea. I was put in the police paddy wagon and then in the Courthouse jail cell (which is underneath the Court House in Washington D.C). My parents were due to arrive the next day, Thursday, for my impending graduation. I was devastated, angry, scared and humiliated. I saw the judge and was released but low and behold, did I not learn my lesson.

Soon after I saw my parents for dinner on Thursday evening, not telling them that I had just got out of jail and been in front of the judge, I went to another graduation party called the pyjama party, which I attend in a negligee. I look back on my behaviour and feel ashamed of it really. Really ashamed of it. But I guess then, we were all just having fun.

At this pyjama party I ran into Stuart, Simon's friend and the one that I went to the Military Ball with. He spoke to me and told me that Simon had apologised to him for getting in the way of Stuart and me getting together. Stuart also told me that Simon would not be coming up for graduation weekend. I was so angry and flew into a silent rage. *How dare Simon think I wanted to be with Stuart and that he got in the way?* Again, just evidence to myself that I could not, nor would I ever, understand Simon's motives, actions and behaviours. We were opposites and from vastly different backgrounds. As I reflect, I possibly need to admit to myself that I was confused about Simon, perhaps that's what it was. He seemed healthy, normal, strong, handsome, charming, fearless, made friends easily, disciplined, knew what he wanted to do with his life. I was none of those things. I felt at the time, I was a reciprocate, not an altruistic being. I think my reciprocity extends from my childhood. But if truth be told, I felt Simon was perhaps emotionally abusive to me and I was blinded by what I thought was love. But it wasn't love, it took me some time to realise that.

My anger turned inward, made me walk away from Stuart and the party. I jumped into my car, under the influence of alcohol along with alcohol and pot in my car and drove towards the police station in Bethesda. Needless to say, I was arrested again. This time, my consequences of my behaviour and actions caused me much more trouble. University Student Affairs got involved and the judge gave me an ultimatum in court, either I go into a drug and alcohol treatment centre or I go to jail for three months. My parents and brother were also hauled up to Student Affairs and that whole thing was humiliating and devastating. I agreed both to the judge in court Friday morning and to Student Affairs that I would attend rehab after my graduation. My father agreed to this and that he would pay for it. It was recommended that I go to the Betty Ford Clinic in California. I just had to wait to get a place sometime in June.

On Saturday at the end of May in 1998, I graduated from a University in Washington DC and I also received an academic award called the RCI Award for International Business. I was grateful to graduate after the trouble I had been in. However, as I reflected on my time at University over the four years, I feel I wasted the experience with a lot of my actions and behaviour. It's not how I thought my university days would go. As I reflect on it now, I wish I had never attended university in the USA and stayed in the UK.

After graduation, I would continue to drink until the day I entered rehab. I knew I was going back to live in England with my parents and start a job with a consulting company and I was sad about this. At the time, I did not want to leave the USA. I wanted to stay. I thought I wanted to become a US citizen. I found the end of my days at University filled with grief and I would cry about this in rehab.

I must point out here that at the time, I thought Simon stole my heart. You know, like when you hear some women talk about the one guy that stole their heart, but they did not end up with. But for me, nowadays, I'm so grateful that I didn't end up with him. I'm grateful to realise that what I experienced with him was not love but lust.

My experiences in my life have taught me that love is something very different, and much greater and I honestly believe it's not something I think I've ever really experienced with a man. I would never see Simon again nor hear from him again until I emailed him in 2013. However, to me, that's not true and I believed, which would be grounded partly with my mental health, that he works in an intelligence agency and that I saw him on the streets of Sydney in 2012 and he was around my life. But I shall get to that much later in my story.

Chapter Eleven
Alcohol and Drug Rehab

It's early June 2018 and my current psychiatrist has added another anti-psychotic to my medications called Latuda. This is because of my issues with voices (although I think many of them are from the brain chip and body possessions). Nonetheless, the suicidal ideation that I tell my psychiatrist about, as I am honest with her, and she lets me know Latuda should help. Latuda is an anti-psychotic for people with bi-polar and Schizophrenia but also acts as an anti-depressant so I am told. It's been one week that I have been taking it as an oral tablet and my suicidal ideation is better, but the depression has not fully lifted yet. After having depression since my teenage years, I wonder if it will ever completely go. Sometimes as I walk around Canberra, I feel heartbroken and frustrated that I cannot view what has happened to me since 2016 (with this brain chip people and these intelligent agency wizards), as a divine spiritual experience and with gratitude, as they showed me so much love and light. But, again, I am getting ahead of myself.

As I lay on the bed in the hotel room in Palm Desert, California in June 1998, waiting for my admittance into the Betty Ford Clinic, I drank. I could not believe my life had come to this, to rehab. I knew little to nothing about the mental illness of alcoholism and addiction and it was hard to accept that I was, and am, an alcoholic. Alcoholism and relapsing have been something that I struggled with, over the decades, and I feel utterly ashamed that at times have not been able to get the AA program.

I am very grateful to my father for providing the excellent education and also paying for my first rehab. The Betty Ford Clinic had not only afforded me an opportunity to get sober but to learn about alcoholism and drug addiction in a safe and secure way. It gave me time and time is what I needed. I would throw myself in to my therapies, lectures and meetings at the Betty Ford Clinic. In some way, I felt I had reached some acceptance that I was an alcoholic but somewhere inside me I felt that wasn't the diagnosis.

Once I completed my thirty days at the Betty Ford Clinic, I returned home to the UK to my parent's house in Wimbledon, to live with them. I did not want to leave the USA, but I had a job starting in London with a consulting company. I continued to go to AA meetings and for the next four years maintained my sobriety, one day at a time.

After starting work with this consulting company, I found it difficult to tell people that I did not drink. This came to fruition in my initial weeks where all the new recruits would have to attend training which was outside Chicago. That's where my fellow new starters would question me on why I wouldn't drink, and I found that to be challenging. Nonetheless, throughout my time at this consulting company I stayed sober, as I did for the following four years, attending AA meetings and working on my recovery.

It was also during this time that I played some golf which my father and mother had been teaching and taking me to lessons for since I was sixteen. I met a golf pro and dated him for six months until I left to go back to the USA. I still remember one of the loveliest things he said to me as he knew I was in AA is that, "Why do bumble bees fly," and he said, "Because they believe they can, Lara. You must believe in yourself." Basically, I was slowly falling apart with bulimia.

It was also during this time that I would seek out my second psychiatrist which I did so at a Hospital in Roehampton UK. He was an Italian psychiatrist and I went to see him stating that I think I am unwell and struggling with depression. He told me there was nothing wrong with me and to get on with my life. I would not seek out a psychiatrist again until I lived in Sydney, twelve years later.

Although my sobriety and AA meetings, along with my first sponsor, helped me to maintain my recovery, other addictions came through namely bulimia. Whilst I was working in Dublin, Ireland for this consulting company I was also bulimic and further diagnosed with Crohn's disease as I was passing so much blood. Steroids were prescribed for me which brought about a significant amount of weight gain. At the end of it all, I could not cope with the working, which was giving me intense anxiety, so I saved up my money to re-admit myself back into rehab for my bulimia. That's how I ended up in my second rehab, in Tucson, Arizona in 1999.

Bulimia is one challenging illness as you become addicted to the eating and purging of food. The purging would give me relief and I could not stop doing it along with barely eating at times, and since I was no longer on the steroids, my weight dropped significantly. After my treatment at Cottonwood, I moved back to Palm Desert, California where I stayed for a month, going to meetings and trying to get on with life. What was even more difficult was that I felt I could not perform with my work, and whilst I was in California, I resigned from this London consulting company. I think my father was very disappointed with me at this time and that I had left England and also left a great job and potential career.

When I reflect on my life, my mental illness and how I have been to my parents and brothers', I imagine it must be so hard for them having me as a child and as an adult daughter. This 'running away' behaviour of mine, so my family called it, would continue decades later also causing more stress and shock for my parents. I have hurt my parents so many times and also said horrible things to my mother when I'm in the height of my illness and I have felt rotten about it. But I will get to that later. For now, it's to know that my behaviour of going back to rehab and then moving to California and eventually settling in San Diego would cause my family problems. Or so I thought. To me, I was causing them stress again.

I had a great AA sponsor at this time who had spent nine months in a rehab after relapsing many times. She lived in Palm Desert, California and when she told me she spent nine months in a US rehab I thought to myself that I hope I didn't have to do that too. For some, alcoholism is a serious, and extremely hard illness to manage one day at a time. Although, at times I have been in good standing with my sobriety, I didn't know that my future relapses and re-entry into AA countless times would be so difficult for me.

In San Diego. I obtained a job which was through a connection I had made in rehab. I worked at an IT company and found a flat to live and continued with my AA program there. During this time, I do not recall having any depression nor did I hear any voices. I worked, caught up with friends and did group therapy with a lovely bunch of people. It was also during this time that I picked up yoga and went regularly, and through this avenue and my group therapy what came up for me, the therapist said, was love addiction. That is to say, I was still pining for love like a lost puppy trying to find his way home. They say Love Addiction is defined as "A compulsive, chronic craving and/or pursuit of romantic love in an effort to get our sense of security and worth from another person." I don't really believe in this definition. For me, my struggle is with where I put and release my love. Nonetheless, it was not so surprising having this come up for me in therapy as I was a romantic back then and had spent my time in my teenage years with my nose in Jane Austin novels. It is something that if I reflect upon now, would be something I would suffer from when I believed in my delusions that all the intelligence agencies, militaries and world leaders would expose me to when they enslaved me in the astral field and had astral sex with me. To me, some of them were suffering from love and sex addiction also. But could that possibly be true?

In San Diego, I ended up meeting a guy who played in a band whose name was Robert. Not much point to go into that relationship though as he told me he was not monogamous, so I ended it. Why he couldn't be honest from the start and tell me he was not monogamous I do not know.

One beautiful experience I did have in California is with an organisation called Women Within. I was fortunate enough to go on an initiation weekend away with them which I loved immensely. It was healing, therapeutic and powerful. The Women Within organisation is something that I do miss, and it is the sister organisation to the Mankind Project, which is also a wonderful organisation for men.

At this IT company, my employer in San Diego, I would meet a client, over the phone as they were in New York, called Adam. Eventually, he would offer me a job in New York City with a new IT start-up that he was joining as CEO. I accepted this opportunity and soon found myself moving to Manhattan in August 2000. My mother visited me in San Diego, before I left for New York, and told me that I would have to accept that her and my father might get a divorce one day. I was shocked and taken aback by her comment but, at the time, thought nothing of it. I just knew I had caused my parents so much stress.

In the California summer heat, after my household goods had been shipped to NY, I boarded a plane and flew to New York City. I had not been to Manhattan since I was with Jack when we spent a weekend there. I was excited. The remnants of the movie *Working Girl* would play through my mind throughout the flight along with the song *Let the River Run* by Carly Simon. Somehow, I felt I had made it; living and working in New York City at 24 years of age.

Chapter Twelve
New York City

It's the 23rd of June 2018 and I have moved into a government housing association one bedroom flat given to me by an ACT Government Housing Association. I am grateful. As I have no possessions, I have inherited furniture and belongings from the former tenant who died here. This is the first time I have lived independently and alone in two years. My depression and suicidal ideation still claw at me like a vicious cat. I attempt mindfulness techniques I learnt in the mental health hospital in Surrey, UK. They work for a short time. Sometimes all I can do is crawl into bed and lie in foetal position and wait for the black dog, as Winston Churchill called it, to pass. I feel lonely and ashamed of my story. Embarrassed to write it, but I want to write it. I let my mind wonder back into its memories of my time in New York. Unafraid of people's judgement of me, I will continue my journey.

As I flew into La Guardia Airport in August 2000 under the hot summer sun; I felt excited and eager to start my new life in New York. Kindly, Adam and the owner of the company, Jon, had arranged for me to stay in Jon's apartment on the upper west side until I obtained my own flat. I was surprised at how expensive apartments were but then again, it was Manhattan and I felt elated. I wondered the streets in the city of lights and got my bearings of where everything was. I went to work on the first Monday with this IT start-up with seed funding called Mobile Media. I was only the fourth employee in New York to join and I joined as their Project Manager. Over the coming year that I was employed with them I watched the company grow, and many more employees joined both in New York and in Finland where there was another office, and where the IT product would be launched.

To explain it better, Mobile Media. had obtained seed funding from a range of investors and was building a product to capture, for example, rates of acquisitions for offline media advertising. The idea was evolutional to me as advertisers often find it difficult to obtain rates of acquisition for example, from their offline media. You must remember this was 2000 and mobile phones were just becoming widely used and based on SMS technology. The idea was that a person could see an AD on TV or in offline media, such as a billboard, and send a message to a particular SMS number to obtain more information. Well this is how I would describe what Mobile Media IT product was doing. Now days of course, you see QR codes on many billboards for example, and scan them quickly with your smartphone. So, the premise of what the investors and Mobile Media were doing was this idea but ten years earlier before QR codes became scan QR codes. Anyway, this is how I would describe it but perhaps Adam or Jon would describe it differently.

I found living in Manhattan fascinating, but I also found the energy very cold. It's so true that it's a city that doesn't sleep but, to me, has very hard energy. It was during my time living in New York that I discovered myself to be empathic and intuitive. I would wonder the streets, shops and bookstores, loved eating in the diner and loved going to the Met and seeing Degas' bronze works and paintings. I felt confident and happy although alone. I dived into attending AA meetings where I met many people which opened my social network and brought me in touch with a women's evening every Friday night. I told no one at work why I didn't drink and as the owner Jon was a Mormon, it was easier to say I just didn't drink.

I worked long hours in New York and I also lost a lot of weight. But, as time went on, I would have a flair up of my Crohn's disease. I managed to find a studio apartment on the upper west side which I loved in a beautiful old building. It was also during this time my depression would creep up on me although I was not taking any medication. Furthermore, I had found MSN chat and started talking to some men from Italy through instant messaging. The first man I met through instant messaging was an Italian man called Robert. We became friends through this way, and I would fly over to Milan, Italy to meet him and his family and stay with them. When I think about how I did this I am shocked at myself as in many ways meeting a man online can be a dangerous thing. However, at the age of twenty-four I was fearless, and it did not bother me to meet someone this way. I only ever saw Robert twice on two separate trips. I enjoyed his company however, as he told me, it wouldn't work, and he was not in love with me. Our friendship ended at Christmas in 2000 and I never really heard from him again.

I did this meet and great online a second time with an Italian called Luke who lived in Rome. To be honest, I am surprised I dated him. He was not my type and we were just friends really, but I did spend time with him both in Italy and in Australia, after I lost my job in New York.

So, to get to that part. Yes, I lost my job in New York. I thought I might as once the company grew the need for me seemed less. It was also my grandfather's 80th birthday and I would miss this as I did not fly home to Australia for it. Basically, I was fired. Being managed out, as they call it, or fired is something that has occurred through many of my employments with various companies. I don't know if it's because they think I am mentally unwell or what, but it is a big part of my journey, continually either leaving jobs or being managed out or fired.

One other important part of my story whilst I was living in New York is that my mother filed for divorce from my father. I would spend much time on the phone with Dad and also, he would come and visit me in New York, and I did my best to console him, support him and love him. I was not shocked that my mother filed for divorce, but I was sad I did not speak to her until my birthday later that year.

As I could not afford to stay in New York after I lost my job, I packed up and moved to Brisbane, Australia to live with one of my brothers for two months until I could figure out what I was going to do. It was at this time that Luke, from Italy, would come to Brisbane and spend a couple of weeks with me as a friend. It was his first trip to Australia, and he enjoyed it very much.

I guess the last thing I need to mention about my time in New York was my extremely slow decent into my mental ill health. New York was the first time I felt paranoid that someone was watching me, namely an intelligence agency. Although that probably sounds like megalomania, it's how I felt. I also felt that something was not right, and I left in August 2001 about two weeks before 9/11. I had packed my things and returned to Australia.

Chapter Thirteen
The Netherlands

It was during my stay at my brothers in Brisbane, along with the savings I had that I agreed to return to Rome, Italy with Luke. So, that's what I did.

I boarded Air Italia in October 2001 and flew back to Rome with Luke. There I found a little apartment to rent and enrolled in intensive Italian class which Luke would take me to each day. I loved Rome and wondering the streets, treating myself to the wonders of Italian food and so much pasta. There, enrolled in intensive Italian classes, I would learn a little of the language which sounded like music to my ears. There were many Korean opera singers in training in my Italian intensive class but what I found out is that I was not very good at learning languages. It is something that did not come to me naturally and I would have to work at it very hard. This is in stark contrast to decades later I felt and had the delusion that I could communicate with alien species very easily. But I will get to that later.

My six weeks that I spent in Rome were so beautiful. I also maintained my sobriety and went to a few AA English speaking meetings which were great. Filled with Americans and I enjoyed hearing their accent again. I realised as I wondered the streets of Rome that Luke and I were just friends and did not have a future, as I knew anyway. Intuition works that way. My mum came over to visit me when it was my birthday in November, and it was after that I returned to London to live with my dad and get a job in the company he worked for. I felt sad leaving Rome, but I jumped on an Air Italia flight and returned to London.

I stayed at my dad's and he helped me get an interview with the company he was Chairman of, a top three world's largest professional services insurance company, along with him being Chairman of Lloyds of London. I was hired as a project manager as they had a goal of building and rolling out a new IT system for the reinsurance operations globally along with, standard business processes. Basically, what was established was an international business analyst team from seven selected countries to determine what the common processes were, and also how a common IT system could be built. In order to do this, I was asked to go and see another business analyst team who were doing a similar project. That's how I met Martin my now ex-husband.

Martin was the project manager working with a business analyst team on the insurance side. They had made a lot of progress and I was sent to meet them in Rome, Italy where they had been gathering requirements. There I met Martin and Emma, the business analyst team leader. I attended one of their meetings and then joined them on the terrace of the hotel for drinks and dinner. It was then I picked up my first drink of alcohol, when I was chatting to Martin, after nearly four years of sobriety. It was April 2002.

My first impressions of Martin were that he was very confident, a bit arrogant and my intuition said for me to stay away from him. But I enjoyed his conversation and he showed me pictures of his parent's farm in South Africa. Martin was South African and lived in Delft, The Netherlands working for this top three international insurance company in Rotterdam. He knew who my father was but was helpful in providing information about their project and how we could do something similar on the reinsurance side.

I had to travel a lot for this job to Paris, Chicago, Hamburg to meet the businesses. I worked with two other colleagues Jeff and Peter to collect requirements and determine what existing IT system could be rolled out or if a new one needed to be built. We held workshops in these countries, and it was on one of these workshops in Paris that I invited Martin down for the weekend before the Monday workshop. It was May 2002 and I had only known Martin for one month before we spent the weekend together and I slept with him and got pregnant with my first child, my beautiful daughter. Not something I intended to happen, but I had been yearning for children. I told Martin I was not on the birth control pill but that didn't seem to matter. Thus, began my five-year relationship and four-year marriage with Martin.

Whilst back in London living at my dad's in June 2002, I was late and took a pregnancy test. It was positive. I called Martin to tell him I was pregnant, and I think he was quite surprised. What was very hard to do was tell my father. But I did. I think he was concerned really, and he ended up calling Martin to London to speak with him. I have no idea what was said in that meeting between my father and Martin, but alas, Martin and I decided to be together and work things out. As a result, by August, I was living in The Netherlands and Martin bought a terrace house in Berkel and Rodenrijs.

We bought some furniture from Ikea and settled into our new home. I took Lamaze classes and also saw the gastroenterologist doctor frequently as my Crohn's disease was flaring up. I was excited to be a mum and Martin and I went and had a 3D scan and found out we were having a daughter. I was so excited. I so wanted to be a mum and have children.

Finding out the sex of our baby helped us plan and buy girl's baby cloths and set-up her room. Throughout this time, I stopped working by November. I resigned from the insurance company and I had thoroughly enjoyed my time working for them. I had a bit of an incident with a friend who asked me how your father feels about having a bastard grandchild. I found this to be very offensive, but I let it go.

For the remanding months of my pregnancy, I stayed at home. On the morning of the 17th February 2003, a large stork was standing on our back garden shed. It was very spiritual to me as if the spirit world and my grandmothers were saying today, she will be born. My contractions started as I stared out the window at this beautiful stork and he turned and flew away. I let Martin know my contractions had started and we called the hospital. I chose a hospital not a home birth. Later that morning we went into the hospital, but I was only three centimetres dilated. No one really explains how painful childbirth is. My labour with my daughter was very long, and it was not until 8.20pm that night that she was born after I had had an epidural. My daughter did not come out crying. She was born, and I held her in my arms, eyes wide open as if to say to the world, *here I am*. I had become a mother and a stay-at-home mum.

I think it is important to note here that although my Crohn's disease had flared up, I did not have any mental health issues except a little bit of depression after my daughter was born. But I heard no voices, had no Schizophrenia. I was utterly in love with my baby daughter and many friends sent flowers and gifts after her birth.

As a new mum, I joined the local ex-pat mothers' group. There I met other mums from Australia, US and England and began my circle of friends. One particular friend, Janie, I became quite close with and she had her daughter after mine. We would go to the playgroups each week and have each other over at our respective homes. I did not speak Dutch, nor did I learn it, which was a bit rude really but so many Dutch people speak English, I was lazy about learning the language.

As my Crohn's disease had flared up again after the birth of our daughter, I had to go back onto the prednisone which is a steroid. As such, I could not continue to breast feed my daughter. We put her onto the bottle, but she had very bad colic and would cry and scream every night for hours. The doctor told me to try goat's milk formulae instead, so that's what we did.

Also, during this time, my mother came to visit. I had missed her over the months although I had been on the phone to her a lot. My father had happily met his new wife, my step-mum who was lovely, and they would come and visit and see their granddaughter along with me going over to London to see them. My relationship with my mother after the birth of my daughter was very special to me as my daughter was the next generation. I would also go over to England to see mum at her house in the countryside with my daughter. My mum very kindly bought me a little Hyundai car, so I could get out and about and get to my mums-and-tots group. Mum was always helping me to make my life easier.

The only issue we had at the time of my daughter's birth was about our marital status. I did not want to marry Martin. I don't really know why I felt that way, I guess I just wasn't big on marriage, but Martin did want to get married otherwise he would not be listed on the birth certificate. I am not sure from Martin's perspective if that was the driver or if he really wanted to marry me. To this day, I do not know. So, two days after my daughter was born, we got married in a civil ceremony at the local authority. Later in the year, we would have our church wedding with friends and family in Australia.

To me, at this time, I was happy. Martin was like a close friend to me and both our relationship and our status as new parents seemed great. We did not fight, and when my daughter was three months old, we travelled to South Africa, so I could meet his parents and introduce them to her. It was a glorious trip spending time in Cape Town and George learning all about his country and culture. I seemed happy and I tried to love Martin.

Chapter Fourteen
Motherhood and Divorce

It's June 28th, 2018. I sit in my community housing flat and it's cold. I have to pay my own electricity and gas bills, but I cannot afford the heating on as I am on $175 a week and I still smoke cigarettes although I know I will quite again. I know my children would be horrified if they knew I was smoking. My motivation and disciple of writing my journey is low and I have to discipline myself to write. I have stopped taking the Latuda today. I let the psychiatrist know. Tomorrow I have my injection. Latuda at 40mg is doing nothing for me. It just makes me feel like throwing up. I sit here and wonder, *Is this story even interesting to anyone? I feel alone, I feel helpless about my future and what I am to do.* Schizophrenia robs you of life. I can only keep going. Fighting for my recovery and stability again. My goal is to finish this memoir. Whatever happens after that I do not know. So, back to my journey.

When my daughter was six months old, in August 2003, I fell pregnant again. I had not been taking any birth control, I was off the prednisone and from what I thought at the time, I wanted a big family. Four or five children. I was twenty-seven years old and pregnant with my second child. Again, we went for a 3D scan and found out it was a boy we were expecting. I was so happy. So was Martin it seemed. I knew he was very keen on having a son. In Martin's family, there is a family bible that's been handed down generation to generation for first-born sons. Now, it would be handed down to our son.

It was also during this time that I planned our wedding. Well, our second wedding. It was held in Queensland; Australia and it was beautiful. We had it at a little country church and our reception at a local restaurant. Family and friends came from all over the world to attend including Martin's parents from South

Africa. I had dreamt and wanted a church wedding if I was to marry at all, and that's what I had, and it was a very special day with my daughter there and me being three months pregnant with our son. I'm grateful to my parents for paying for our wedding. We had our honeymoon at Port Douglas and then flew back to The Netherlands for Christmas. I have kept my wedding photos which are in a trunk stored away at my Aunt's farm.

On Monday the 19th April 2004, I awoke and saw again, another stork standing on the back shed in the garden. Again, a stork was standing tall as if to signal to me from the spirit realm the birth of my son that day. As it flew away, my contractions started and at 5.10pm that afternoon I gave birth to our son. He came out screaming like most babies do. I was now the proud mother of two little angels. I was so happy. My daughter had a brother and she was just fourteen months old when he was born.

Unlike my daughter who did not sleep as much and had colic, my son slept nearly sixteen hours a day and had no colic. I breast feed him until he was four months old and although it was a lot of work having two children close together, it was blissful.

When I reflect back on my time being a mother, I am not sure if I was a good one. I gave birth to two very active, sassy and strong children and I would sometimes not cope as well as I think I should have. But I will get to that later.

I enjoyed being a stay-at-home mother and Martin was a good provider. The stress of not having to work and to have the ability to stay at home and raise children I was grateful for.

As the children grew, Martin and I would begin discussing where we wanted to live. As I did not speak Dutch and the children were not learning it either, I would press Martin that we had to move either to England, Australia or the USA. Thus, began his search for employment in an English-speaking country. I had always known since I first met Martin that he wanted to live in Chicago. I am not sure why at the time, but I was less interested in living there and wanted the children to be raised in the UK. So, in 2005, Martin conceded, and we moved to Australia where he would work for an insurance company in Sydney. I knew Martin was unhappy with this. I too could see it was and possibly felt like a career-limiting move and I realised during our six months in Sydney, it appeared, Martin was not happy working there. I wasn't happy in Australia either. In

October 2005, a month before my thirtieth birthday, Martin went on assignment to Chicago and eventually secured a job there with an insurance company. So, in December 2005, I moved, with the children, to Chicago and it was so cold.

During my time in Sydney 2005 and again in Chicago, I would seek out clairvoyants. I am a firm believer in the spirit realm and there are some, like John Edwards, who can bring messages through from loved ones that had passed. I used to talk to Martin about this also. Whilst we lived in Sydney, I saw two clairvoyants, one of whom let me know I would be moving from Sydney and that, one day, I would have a large legal battle. It was in this message that the clairvoyant told me I would meet my future husband after this legal battle once I have stood in my power. I was surprised by this message since I was already married. However, it would be the same sentiment that a clairvoyant in Chicago would tell me.

It was in my first meeting with this clairvoyant in Chicago where she said you cannot leave Martin yet, but you will. This, she said, was the messages from my grandmothers who she brought through. She also said I could be clairvoyant, but I needed training which she did. I guess if I was honest with myself, I had thought about leaving Martin. I think we both knew our relationship was starting to fall apart and we either needed to focus on getting it back on track or we would end up in divorce. Also, Martin seemed unhappy with me along with withdrawn from me and seemed angry. I seemed withdrawn and angry. But still we kept going.

I think it was in January 2006, Martin and I bought a beautiful big six-bedroom home in the suburbs of Chicago. It was like a dream come true and could have been our forever house had I stayed in the marriage. However, our relationship still appeared to be treading on broken glass. I did not want to be with him. Emotionally, mentally, spiritually and sexually I was dissatisfied and felt incomplete. I remember when we went to make the down payment on the house with the real estate agent and the lawyers, we were standing in the driveway with the children and I had forgotten to bring the $55,000 check with me from the apartment in Chicago. Martin appeared to be upset with me that I had forgotten to bring the check. My daughter fell over and bumped her head and a large swelling occurred, and I had to take her to the hospital emergency room, so we were late to the lawyers. She ended up with a black eye but no damage. I thought then, that Martin was not happy and always getting angry with me.

I recall two other things that bothered me in Chicago which I told Martin about. The first is that I joined a yoga school and I was having a massage there and the instructor straddled my hand and placed his balls in my fingers. I was so shocked and moved my hand away. Secondly, the gardener who used to do our garden around the house asked if I wanted a massage and if he could come into the house and do that for me. I was revolted. I mention these things because later this sexual inappropriateness from men would become a humongous issue in the decade ahead, particularly as a single mother.

I did talk to my mother a bit about my wanting to divorce. She would call me from the UK, and I would discuss it with her I was unhappy, and she knew that. She was so supportive of me on the calls and as any mother feels for her daughter, she just wanted me to be happy. I felt like a frozen bird in my marriage, slowly being starved of love.

It was Christmas 2006 and one of my brothers came over from Australia and bought with him the Secret DVD. Here I learnt about the law of attraction. It was then, I was determined to divorce. We then flew together for two weeks holiday to my mother's in the UK and I asked her if I could see her lawyer that she used in her own divorce from my father. He would refer me to a divorce attorney in Chicago.

When I returned from the UK, I did not go and see this divorce attorney until after my daughter's birthday, I think. It took me time to think and make the final decision to divorce. Furthermore, Martin knew I had seen a divorce lawyer as he saw my email open and had read emails from the lawyer. After this incident of my emails being read, I went and saw this lawyer, with my mother providing the retainer, and I filed for divorce.

I also heavily saw the clairvoyant in Chicago during this time. As she brought my grandmothers through and others in the spirit realm, she told me I would be getting divorced and that I would meet a James Bond type referring to Roger Moore in the James Bond film Octopussy, who would be my future partner. This must sound insane to say but that is what happened.

Nonetheless, I would never meet this James Bond and both myself and my children would miss out on his guidance, love, loyalty, happiness and fun.

One other thing I did after learning about the law of attraction was to do a vision board session with a group of people. Vision boards are something they mention in the Secret DVD based upon the law of attraction. I mention this because of one thing I stuck on my vision board. It was the words 'fight for your human rights'. I have no idea why I did that but to me, the law of attraction would work on those words and over the next decade I would have to fight for my human rights on an extreme level or so I felt.

Lastly, it was also during this time that I picked up and felt that intelligence agencies were around my life. I guess a psychiatrist may call that a delusion and Schizophrenia but that is what I felt. When I reflect on it now, I guess I can say that my mental health was starting to crack. Why did I think intelligence agencies were around my life? But that's what I thought. I guess if the judge had known that I was thinking this, I would not have obtained custody of my children.

After a few court appearances regarding my divorce and removing my children to the UK or Australia, the judge granted me custody of the children and the ability to leave the US. What was complex is that I would lose my US visa once divorced, I was told and therefore, I had no choice but to leave the US although I wanted to. Martin did not attend any of the divorce hearings, and on the 7th March 2007, my divorce was granted.

As I packed up to leave with our children, the home was rented out for two years and Martin moved into an apartment in Chicago. I could see Martin's pain, hurt and anguish. He was broken regarding losing our children and my moving away. Martin dropped the children and me off at the airport and we flew to London to my mother's. Little did I know the next chapter of my live would expose me to experiences I could not have comprehended, seen coming or thought possible.

Chapter Fifteen

Single Mum and Australia

There is nothing like flying into the UK. The quaint English housing lining the streets and the delicious green countryside are both beautiful to look at. When I divorced from Martin, my daughter was four years old and my son was two, about to turn three years old. On a sun-drenched morning in March 2007, we landed at London Heathrow airport and my mother picked us all up. We went back to her house and I stayed with her practically for a month. During this time, she talked to me about returning to Brisbane, Australia to settle with the children.

I have to admit here that I felt intelligence agencies were in and around my life at this time. I don't know why I thought that, but I did. To a psychiatrist, this would mean that my mental health was slowing deteriorating, but to me, the intelligence agencies surrounding my life were very real.

Regardless, after an effort to see if I could settle in London which could have worked for me, my mother and I discussed me returning to Australia, and I ended up moving back to Brisbane, Australia in April 2007. My mother had arranged for me to stay with old family friends who very kindly took us in. Thus, began my Australia journey.

I knew I would have to return to work even though Martin was paying me decent child support. So, I enrolled the children in day-care and began seeking out employment. Before I left London, I saw an old friend of my brothers who worked at a recruitment company. Thus, with his referral I was able to contract with them in Brisbane for three months. As a result, my first employment was with a bank on a three-month contract whilst I looked around for permanent employment. I found a three-bedroom home in Brisbane to live in and household possessions had been shipped from Chicago. The children and I settled into our new life and they Skyped with Martin, my ex-husband, twice a week.

I found working in Brisbane culturally challenging. I had spent my entire adult life thus far in the USA or UK along with The Netherlands and had not really lived in Australia since those six months in Sydney with Martin. I found the Australian culture in Brisbane to be sexist and vastly different from working overseas. Nonetheless, I continued to seek out permanent employment.

It was during this time that I met up with my friends from my old High School where I went as a young teenager. It had been about fourteen years since I had seen them, but I caught up with Petra, Edith and Rebecca to name a few.

It was through Edith that I would be referred to a job at a top five world's largest professional services consulting company. After a four-stage interview process, I was successful and, thus in August 2007, my employment with this consulting company began.

My life became very full. Working full time for this firm and raising two adorable young children. At times I reflect on this, as I have grown older, how being able to be a stay-at-home mum would have been so much better. I missed my children whilst at work and was grappling with my experiences as a young mother.

To all intents and purposes, I must write about my experiences at this consulting company despite the fact they could sue me, I guess.

I was employed as a senior manager in this consulting company. I had bought expensive cloths and suits for work and many high-heeled shoes. This was made possible by a bank which had given me a $30,000 credit card.

I had professional photographs taken of myself and always acted with professionalism. At the time, this consulting company had a big pitch going to secure a multi-year project with a health department. We were all busy preparing the proposal and conducting interviews and workshops with the Health organisation staff. The contract was won by this consulting company, but I started to notice things were not going well for me there.

Whilst I was working there, my mother moved down to Kogan in Australia. There she would sometimes take my children for the weekend and give me a break. It was through her doing this that I would go out with friends or for dinner and I was drinking alcohol. I never drunk through my pregnancies and my alcoholism had not taken off. It seemed moderate if nothing at all.

One evening after a dinner with colleagues, one of my colleagues (and I cannot remember his name) said he would take me home first in a taxi. Once we arrived at my house, and the children were not there on this occasion but with my mother, he tried to kiss me and told me 'I would feel better after I had sex' with him. He was married, and I was shocked, turned him down and asked him to leave. I ended up telling Edith this who was a manager at the company and an old school friend. What I didn't realise is this would end up being gossiped and spread about and cost me my employment. Basically, I guess someone construed it as sexual harassment and this organisation already had a large sexual harassment case going with a former employee.

Before I started to feel the effects of being managed out by this company, a number of other things happened. Firstly, one sunny morning when I was walking into work with Edith, I told her I had Crohn's disease. As a qualified doctor she told me, "People with Crohn's disease are fucked in the head." I was so shocked at her response to me, but it made me realise she was also part of the movement in this organisation that was trying to manage me out. Or was my perception changing and my mental health deteriorating?

Secondly, I was assigned a piece of work for a real estate company, the client being a real estate mogul. After doing the proposal, I met with him and the partner I worked for. I could tell this was a very sexually charged meeting and this real estate mogul took off his wedding ring and looked at me and said, "What happens in Vegas stays in Vegas." But what I have to admit here is that I remembered this real estate mogul from my childhood as we went to the same primary school for a time and he lived around the corner from me. Furthermore, I must mention that I thought I fell for him. I was instantly attracted to him and thought I fell in love with him. But again, it was lust not love. But strangely in a way, to me, I felt like I was being set-up.

This real estate mogul didn't want to work with me or perhaps it was my boss who didn't want me to work with him, so another male colleague was assigned. I simply managed the budget and noticed on one occasion that this real estate mogul, had been over charged. I raised this with my boss, but to no avail. It would not be long before I was managed out even when I had networked with other colleagues in Sydney.

Being managed out of a job is an awful experience. First, people stop talking to you and treat you as though you do not belong in the job. Next, they start on your performance even after positive evaluations, all of a sudden, your work and performance is not up to scratch. Then comes the ignoring you and not giving you any work or giving you too much work that is unachievable. But at this company I again started to feel that intelligence agencies were watching me and had me under some type of surveillance. I guess with the stress of everything, my mental health was starting to crack.

In January 2008, just as my daughter started Prep School, I was called by one of my colleagues and told that I needed a lawyer. I asked why I needed a lawyer and he implied that I would be let go. I had already been put on some type of probation despite being part of the Health pitch which was estimated to make the company over $80 million. If I recall correctly, even the CEO of the company in New York sent a letter to us all congratulating us on the win.

I spoke with my friend Petra who was also a lawyer and she recommended one to me. So, I contacted him and told him what was going on. We had to meet with the company's lawyers who were ferocious, and it was advised to me that I should resign. So, I did. I had only been employed at this company for six months.

By February 2008, I was unemployed. I cried. Working in corporations is a lot more challenging than I thought. A man at the real estate company where the real estate mogul worked contacted me and arranged for me to meet with this real estate mogul and thus, I flew down to Sydney to meet him for coffee and interview for other jobs. He is a very charming man and I was confused with the feelings I had for him. Moreover though, I felt autistic as I did not pick up on the social ques. He had a job available as an executive assistant and I think he was trying to ascertain whether I wanted that. It was not until after our coffee that I had these thoughts. But I felt insulted that all he thought I wanted to be an executive assistant. I'd worked all over the world, it didn't seem right to me.

A friend of mine in Brisbane recommended a clairvoyant to go and see and that is when I met Jude. I saw her twice and she indicated that I would be moving to Sydney and had a new job coming through.

I had applied to a job at another top five global consulting company in Sydney and, after four interviews, I was successful. So, in April 2008, I packed up and had everything shipped and drove with my children down to Sydney to Millers Point near The Rocks. There was a local school there for my daughter and a day-care centre for my son. It was a three-bedroom two-storey apartment and it was just perfect. My time in Sydney with my children would challenge me and my mental health started to deteriorate further. But, moreover, I would feel that there were many intelligence agencies from across the world, along with militaries that would begin to terrorise me and use certain weaponry to harm me. But, to explain that, I would need to discuss PSYOPs and war games along with, electromagnetic military weaponry; none of which I understand.

Chapter Sixteen
Sydney, Australia

It's been three weeks since I have written. I stand, after my shower, naked in front of the bathroom mirror. My body is unrecognisable to me. My arms, legs and buttocks are like bubble wrap, indented here and there with cellulite. My stomach is a mixed bag of bulging fat. Thirty kilos I have put on and I do not know who I am anymore or who is in this body. I grabble with the basic self-care that doctors mention with people with mental ill health. I used to shower every day, keep my house clean and tidy. But nowadays it's an effort to shower, so I do it every second day. It's an effort to shave my legs, so I resort to doing it once a week. My kitchen is a mess, dishes piled up ready for washing. I am a skeleton of my former self. I struggle with understanding the point of my existence. My Crohn's disease (inflammatory bowel disease) has flared up. So, I start taking my Crohn's disease medication again; Imuran and Asacol. Imuran can cause pancreatic cancer and skin cancer. I wonder what the point is. What is the point of my continued existence?

My thoughts and feelings seem selfish to me. I am not homeless but in a government community flat. I am not starving in the streets of Africa or India. I had good times in my life that I can reflect upon and enjoy the sweet memories and feelings that they bring. It's the future I don't understand. Plus, what I need to write unveiling the twisted depth of my mental illness, like peeling off a facial mask. It's humiliating in a way and I feel ashamed of my Schizophrenia. But I want to write even though I am not a good writer. After my copious mental health hospital admissions (seven in fact), sometimes, I turn the radio on and dance in my living room in an effort to change my mood. Something I learnt from the UK mental health hospitals. It helps. Dancing. But, back to my days in Sydney.

When I left this consulting company in February 2008, (well what I call managed out), I had to sign a legal contract stating something about not being able to sue this organisation or testify in any court regarding them. Well, that's the gist of it to me, but honestly, I cannot remember the details of it.

In April 2008, I settled my children into school and day-care respectively and began working at this next global consulting company. I had arranged for an au pair to help me with the children and collect them from school and day-care. Our first au pair was from Paris and lived with us for six months before a new au pair would come. I would stay with this consulting company for three years and I enjoyed my time with them and my colleagues and work associates. I was hired as a senior manager in consulting, but as time went on with them, things would become strange and my mental health worse. It was during these years that I felt intelligence agencies and militaries would surround me along with a drug cartel. I felt terrified of my thoughts.

I loved living in Sydney. The weather is perfect and our little three-bedroom two-story flat in Kent Street in Millers Point was homely. I loved raising my kids and, each night, I would tuck them up and read them bedtime stories. My children were a joy to raise but I do not wish talk too much about them other than how they were impacted by what was going on around me and with me.

It appeared to me during this time in 2008 that this real estate mogul and others, including my friends, were surrounding my life and trying to set me up with him. I noticed on my way back from work (I used to walk to and from work) that I was under surveillance. By this I mean, men and women standing at certain corners, sometimes holding a newspaper, until I got home safely from work. I did not understand what was going on, but I felt I was like in some kind of movie with either an intelligence agency or a private security firm had me under watch. It was also during this time that I believed my house to be bugged by intelligence agencies and the militaries. These thoughts are what psychiatrists refer to as delusions.

I also felt that this real estate mogul was stalking me. He would drive by my flat or sometimes seem to accidently run into me in Double Bay (a Sydney suburb). This stalking, or what I considered to be stalking, set-off my mental health in terms of severe anxiety. I would think to myself why does he stalk me but not talk to me? Throughout my time in Sydney I would go to AA meetings off and on but all I felt was that others were watching me. One particular man introduced himself to me and said he was from a military and I could not understand why anyone from any military would be involved in my life.

It was during the early part of my time in Sydney that I would have, what I believe, to be my first psychotic break. What I need to state though is that my mental health and ill health, was sporadic and I was not always unwell but sporadically unwell. I was driving the car with the children home from Bondi and I felt something snap in my brain and my mind and body were awash with severe anxiety. It was as if my mind had caved in and started to not function properly. I felt terrified. I couldn't sleep as I would lay awake with anxiety each night. I went to see the doctor (GP) and he proscribed me Valium. No further referral to mental health was made.

However, I still made new friends in Sydney one of which was a friend from the consulting company we worked at together. Her and her husband and children would invite us to go camping together, sometimes to the beach and sometimes to the forest. The children and I had a wonderful time with them and their support and kindness to me and the children was so welcomed. However, I still had thoughts that I was being stalked and people were trying to set me up with a real estate mogul.

One night in August 2008, I went out to the Ivy Bar in Sydney with my old school friend. I had the thought that she had been talking with this real estate mogul and was trying to set me up with him. Also, at the Ivy Bar, I noticed a lot of men about, keeping me under surveillance. I met this real estate mogul at the Ivy, towards the end of the night, and went home with him for what is called a one-night stand. He did not meet me to ask me out for a date; it was a one-night stand. We went back to his apartment in Sydney and had some champagne on his balcony. I was riddled with anxiety and not even the sweet taste of the champagne could calm me. We went into his bedroom and started kissing. I guess I do not need to go into the details about it, but sex hurt with him that night. I could not get aroused and I could not stop my anxiety from debilitating me. I left in the wee hours of the morning back to home to the au pair who had been looking after my children. It is this sexual experience with this real estate mogul that would get men talking and thereafter, I would become, to me, a victim of gross sexual harassment and exploitation by intelligence agencies and military personnel later on but, in a way, I could not have fathomed.

It was also during 2008 that the Australian Federal Police (AFP) would meet us out at the bar downstairs near my employer's office. It was Friday night and two Australian Federal police officers would introduce themselves to me and some of my colleagues whom I was having a drink with. I asked them, "Can I see your AFP badge," and they showed me. I joked with them saying, "Oh, are you like the FBI?" They were both drinking coke and no alcohol. They followed us to the next bar, and I remember their faces distinctly. I was wondering to myself, why was the AFP at the bar and chatting to me? Was I in some sort of trouble? Well, those are the thoughts I had. I remember these two AFP officers because months later, they would appear at the local police station when I was there.

For Christmas 2008, my mother came down to spend it with the children and me. It was then, when we were at the Bondi mall, that I passed a pet shop and saw Cavoodle puppies there. I would later discuss that with my mum and go back to Bondi to buy a Cavoodle puppy for my children's Christmas present. We named him Toby and I loved him dearly.

I filled the weekends with the children with soccer during the winter and swimming lessons and nippers (on the beach), during the summer. Sydney beaches are so beautiful, and both my children loved playing on the beach and in the park.

In 2009, there seemed to be the opinion in Sydney, although I probably sound like a megalomaniac saying it, that something was wrong with my sexuality as I was not having sex and one-night stands like other people. In March 2009, Tim came into my life and I met him at a bar downstairs at World Square.

Tim would talk to me about how he was a Freemason (as if I was meant to be impressed by this) and that he swam the English Channel. That was impressive. The night we met at the bar he would talk to me about things and that we would date. He also said to me, "People's power is crashing into each other, Lara." To me, he seemed to have been placed in my life for a

86

reason and that sex was a large part of that. He implied that someone had to sleep with me because I was not having sex. To fast forward this whole process I would just get to the point with him about it and he invited the children and me over to stay one night. Tim's sex was sort of similar to something like the movies and books *Fifty Shades of Grey* without all the equipment. He could also multi orgasm and I have to say I faked everything with him and pretended to orgasm. I don't know why I did this; lie I mean about pleasure. But I did.

He suggested the next time that he stay over at my place which we did, and it is then that I believe I was being watched and videoed and that the first sex tape by spy agencies was made of me. But I have no evidence of this. Alas, this would be construed as a severe delusion. Being videoed I mean because I thought my house was bugged by intelligence agencies.

On one occasion I was driving Tim back to his house and he said, "You just need to look pretty and suck cock, Lara." I couldn't believe I was being spoken to in this way and that that was the sentiment of the men in Sydney about me. Tim also told me that I had 'saggy breasts' and that would trigger a great deal of hurt in me and also activate me to consider breast implants.

That Easter holidays, as Tim and my three-month relationship was coming to an end; as I believe he was told to break up with me. Thank goodness. Nonetheless, I used my credit card and took my children on holiday to Fiji. We had a fantastic time and Fiji has such beautiful energy. After I got back, Tim and I were over. I felt like I had passed the sex test they were putting me under.

By mid-2009, I was sitting in my room one weekend sorting out the clean laundry and I had an overwhelming urge to stab and mutilate my vagina. I was tired of the stalking, tried of people taking pictures of me out in public, tired of the sexual harassment, tired of my friends telling me I was going to get married soon. The urge was sudden, abrupt and terrifying. I had never been a self-harmer, but this urge was strong. The only way men would leave me alone, I thought, was to stab my vagina and mutilate it. I stood in my room and took some deep breaths and thought to myself, *what could I do?* Were they using weapons on me? Were they doing this to me? My mental health was deteriorating, gripping me like a steal clamp.

Chapter Seventeen
A Business Tycoon

If I can recall correctly it was sometime in 2009 that I would email a business tycoon at his company in Australia. I sent him at the info email, my resume seeking employment. I have to honestly ask myself why I did this. To be honest, I wanted him to find out who was stalking me, and why I was under surveillance from intelligence agencies and militaries.

I was writing a diary during these years and I did write that I loved this business tycoon. I don't know why I felt love for him. I thought I wanted to be with him and also people would talk to me about him. I guess, I wanted his marriage to break up. Wanted him to reveal in the media why this was happening to me. I wanted him to determine why was some type of military or electromagnetic weaponry was being used on me, causing me to have severe brain stem pain. I wanted him to find out why they were using PSYOPs on me and what the hell was going on? Selfishly, I wanted his protection and in my delusion about who he was, to report it to the media.

In my delusions, I believe intelligence agencies and militaries, used certain weaponry on me which was causing severe brain stem pain in me and deteriorating my mental health rapidly. To me, this went on in 2009, 2010 and 2011. I do not know much about what this weaponry is. I guess I could research it, but I consider what's the point? Did people know it was happening? I even had delusions about my parents, and I believed, they were spoken to by intelligence agencies although they never admitted this to me. It was so sad to me that I would think this about my parents, and I felt scared.

I only ever said hello to this business tycoon once and that was down at the beach when our children were on a train ride.

Besides that, my son was in the same nipper's group as his son. I said hello to him, but I was too shy to talk any more than that.

I think it was 2009 that one of my University friends came down to Sydney for her honeymoon. I also had the thought and feeling that she had been talking with the real estate mogul and was part of setting me up on the street with him on my birthday in 2009.

I also believed at the end of 2009 on my birthday, a colleague at the company I worked for, would also try and set me up on the street with this real estate mogul and this is what happened. My University friend sent me an email asking, 'am I ready?' Ready for what I did not know. I left work early that day and, as I was walking home, the real estate mogul and his project manager from a company he was working with, stood on the street waiting for me. I said hello and had a little chat. Little did I know that I felt my employer was trying to manage me out and the real estate mogul wanted to offer me a job. Well, that's how I see it. I said goodbye and walked home.

By 2010, I had noticed the following spies in Sydney along with, the fact that, they started using the real estate mogul look-alikes on me. Basically, what this means is that as I would walk to work, a real estate mogul look-alike would be passing me on the street and staring at me. This impacted my mental health greatly. As an empath, I can pick up spies quite easily although a psychiatrist would call that a delusion. I felt there were so many spies in Sydney. Why I was under this surveillance has never been explained to me and I guess never will be. Basically, it's all called delusions by doctors but to me, my delusions were real.

One afternoon on the way home from work, one of my school friends' mums', said to me, "Why don't you go to the media?"

I said, "I don't know how." She warned me the Police were standing up on the road ahead of me with machine guns. I started to cry. I carried on past them to collect my children from afterschool care. I felt like the Police were trying to intimidate me.

It was also in 2010, I met with a colleague who told me, "The only way for justice, Lara, is to write a book." These comments from people made me realise that a lot of people knew what was going on, but no one was telling me the truth. Behind it all I thought it was intelligence agencies and militaries. Sometimes, I thought it was my old University fling, Simon, who I deluded myself into believing was a spy.

In 2010, whilst I was in AA and not drinking, I walked home and my grandmother apparitioned in front of me. Not many people believe in the spirit realm but that is what happened to me and it gave me the fright of my life.

I had set up some appointments via the telephone to Jude, the physic from Brisbane and also the clairvoyant from Chicago. In the appointment with Jude, she told me I would be the head harem in Sydney, I was so angry and devastated that she said this, and it indicated to me that I was surrounded by men and a harem. It was also during this time that I learnt that the real estate mogul had a son from another relationship and had not told me this. On another call with clairvoyant from Chicago, she brought through the most profound message of all, "Lara, you do not owe anyone anything."

On my final call with the clairvoyant from Chicago, she told me "get your shit together or he is not coming in." To me this was in reference to a business tycoon or the real estate mogul. All I saw when she said this was a sea of black. I felt scared. I didn't know how to *get myself together* when I felt I was falling apart.

At some point during this time, I ended up going to the Police station that was down the road from where I lived. I went because I was tired of being stalked and tired of what was going on. The two Australian Federal Police officers that I had met at the bar and chatted too, turned up and went into another room. There was also a lady there who I thought was a spy. I was questioned, even asked if my brothers would take bribes and I discussed with them what I thought was going on. I knew the AFP officers were watching. To no avail, I left the police station. They could do nothing.

As my mental health started to deteriorate more, I ended up seeing a GP who told me, "They are trying to control you, Lara." Who is trying to control me and what is the point of that? Still to this day, I do not know. But it was then that I would see a Sydney psychiatrist. He was known as the psychiatrist for the wealthy and so-called famous people of Sydney. However, I cannot remember his name. To me, he would be very unprofessional and asked me questions about my employers and about VIPs. I found the appointments useless. One time, he asked me out to dinner which I agreed to and we went on his scooter down to his flat in Woolamaloo. That night, at dinner he told me that I cannot contract HIV unless I am on my period. I could not believe the conversations he would have with me and the ridiculousness of his words. I stopped seeing him and got on with my life. It was also about this time that I stopped having au pairs at home and picked the children up myself from after school care.

Throughout 2010, I believed that a military was entering my home and reading my diary. I could tell just by my dog Toby who was cowering every time I came home. In 2010, a colleague asked me what I thought of another VIP and if I liked him. I didn't understand why any VIP would be interested in me. I knew I was struggling with my mental health and I also believed I was surrounded by intelligence agencies.

It was also in 2010 that my grandfather (my mother's father) became very ill and was put onto palliative care. I was working on a client site, a bank, and my step-grandmother called me to tell me Granddad did not have long to live. Martin and his new wife were due to come down to Sydney to visit the children, but I had to change the dates so that the children and I could get up to Queensland to visit Granddad and that's what we did. During my visits with him, I would place hands over his chest trying to bring down the light to relieve the congestion in his chest. It was something that I learnt in Sydney when I went to a meditation and channelling light session with a lady who worked for John of God from Brazil. Six months later, my granddad died at age 89. Even though I didn't spend much time with him in my adult life, I would miss him greatly.

Chapter Eighteen
My Geographicals

It has been four years and five months since I have last seen my children. I miss them dearly and dream of them at night. My ex-husband Martin will not send me any photos of them, so I do not know what they look like as they grow up. As the August winter approaches in Canberra 2018, I wonder to myself when and if I will ever see them. I have no money to go there. All I can do is pray they are happy and well.

In the news, there is continued talk of countries hacking and interfering in the 2016 US Presidential election. I agree. In my severe delusion, I felt I had something to do with it, as at the time, someone hacked my brain interface (brain chip), merged with my body in some spiritual attack and pulled my abdominal wall through the astral field. It is so hard to explain this stuff and only those who do it or some intelligence agents and military personnel would understand. But again, I am getting ahead of myself and I need to get back to my time in Sydney in 2010.

At the end of 2010, the owner of the three-bedroom apartment we lived in would inform me through the real estate agent that we would have to move. This was unsettling, and I felt very worried. I managed to find a two-bedroom apartment in Elizabeth Bay close to the park. It was awful in comparison.

I had the feeling, well as it's called delusions, that the children and I were surrounded by spies, by intelligence agencies from across the world. I told my children about this which was wrong. But I was terrified. Why were all these intelligence agents surrounding us? Even a walk in Elizabeth Bay park, there would be spies around us. One of them screamed at me in the park. Why was I being yelled at by a man in the park, who I thought was a spy?

At Christmas 2010, I took the children up to the Sunshine Coast in Queensland, so they could see their cousins and Pop (my father) and my stepmother. It would be the last time my family, children and I would be together. My life would take a downward spiral and my mental health would rapidly deteriorate. It was also at this time and since 2009, that I thought a business tycoon was stalking me and had my mobile phone hacked. One particular experience was that he appeared on the Sunshine Coast that Christmas and I saw him in the car park at the beach when I was walking my dog Toby. I told my friend this and he just said, "Well, this tycoon is gone now." Why would no one tell me the truth?

I noticed also the mental health of my children being impacted by what was going on around me and in my life. My daughter came home one afternoon from after school care with 'Witch' written on her hand and filled with anxiety in her eyes. My son's legs were covered in bruises and he told me he was getting kicked at school. I felt I could not protect my children and felt we were being terrorised. I did not know what to do.

As I sat with my children watching the fireworks dancing across the night sky on New Year's Eve in Sydney, I wondered to myself what 2011 would bring. I started to communicate to my mother more and she suggested that I move to England and live near her. Well, I think that is what she suggested. At work, they started to call me Princess, and I had the delusion that that was something to do with another VIP. On one afternoon in Elizabeth Bay Park, an older gentleman came up to me and started chatting to me. He quoted some book about me being a whore and told me what men had said about me that 'her pink stuff is good, but her head is fucked'. I felt isolated and alone.

Alas, in March 2011, I decided to move from Sydney to my mother's in England. So, I packed us all up, got rid of a lot of belongings and household furniture and arranged for Toby, our dog, to be brought to England also. My mother was there at Heathrow airport waiting for us and I felt relieved. Relieved to be near mum again and relieved to be in the UK. But I still had delusions that spies, were talking to my mother. This made me feel sad.

As I resigned from working at the consulting company in Australia, I had to apply for jobs in England and ended up getting a job with the Global company in London. It would mean I would need to commute to London from Surrey. I enrolled both my children into a private school, in Godalming, Surrey.

My ex-husband's emails became more difficult for me and I would have the delusion that it was either his lawyer or an intelligence agency that was writing them. He was not happy that the children were enrolled in a private fee-paying school and wanted them to attend the government state school. This would eventually happen.

On one occasion when my mother brought my daughter and son up to London to see me at lunchtime from work, I was standing waiting for them outside Embankment Tube station and looked to the roof on the left. There was a massive camera taking photos of me and I did not know why. Somehow, it felt to me, the media was now also all around me and the photographs both from civilians and the media occurred.

Throughout 2011, I was riddled with anxiety. I kept going to the GP, but to no avail. It was although I would just have to suffer through it. Once, I took the children to the Ascot horse races and a man screamed at me, "You should not be alone." Clearly, a warning I could not understand.

As I became more unwell, I thought that it was not going to work living with my mother and I could not work full time, commute to London and get the children from after school care. But this thought was wrong. My mother was supportive and always helpful, and I should have just found a flat to live in. That frustrates me. What I did next.

Again, I would do geographical and take the children back to Sydney, Australia in January 2012. On one occasion my boss at this consulting company in London, said to me, "Why do you shine the light on dark places?" Another colleague said she knew a hitman who could deal with my ex-husband. All I could think to myself was what is going on?

As I was travelling home one day on the train from Waterloo, I was being watched by a man who was smiling at me and being empathic, I felt he was an IRA terrorist. Well, that's the energy I picked up anyway. So now to me, I was somehow surrounded by terrorists. Hard to believe I know, but this terrorism would get even worse in 2016.

So, in January 2012, I told my mother the children and I would move back to Australia with Toby. Little did I know how difficult it would be to get Toby back into Australia and he had to stay in quarantine for six months.

These geographicals, I know impacted my children as I was not providing a stable environment for them anymore. But, returning to Sydney and to their old school and after-care gave them some kind of continuity. From the money I had saved from working in London, I was able to find a two-bedroom unit in Milsons Point just near the Sydney Harbour Bridge. Well, I only had money to pay for two months. I did not know what to do because after that time, and without me having a job, we would be homeless.

I cannot say my time in Sydney was any better. Tinted window cars kept stalking me and watching me. One morning when I was taking the children to school, there was a tied roll of string on the pavement and I tripped on it and cut open my knee. To me it was planted there by an intelligence agent. I had to go to hospital with the children and get a stich. One of the other things I found strange is that the Police (and even Police in England) would always be around when I felt some guy was stalking me. Sometimes he was on a motor bike, other times in a pub. Moreover, once when I was sitting at Starbucks after I had dropped the children at school, someone was sitting behind me and stuck some taser thing in my back which really hurt. I reported it to the Police, but nothing came of it.

At one stage, one of the mothers at the children's school asked me, "Do you know who is doing this to you?"

I said, "No, but I thought it was a VIP or an intelligence agent." But I knew that was wrong. To me, it felt like a terrorist.

She said, "We will say a prayer to have him leave you alone." Thus, together on the streets of Sydney we prayed to God that whoever this man was, he would leave me alone. However, to me, that prayer was unanswered.

As time grew close to an end on our two-bedroom flat, homelessness was staring me in the face. I had not succeeded in getting a job and had nowhere for the children and me to live. Fortunately, one of the mothers from the children's school spoke to me and she offered us to live with her and I could rent a room until I got a job and a place to live. So, in March 2012, I moved in with Emily and her husband Casper. It was not easy.

Emily and I would talk, and she said, "Why don't you send the children to live with their father in the US." I was upset with this and said, "I didn't want to lose my children."

One night on the computer, the words streamed across the screen 'stop fighting' and Casper came rushing down to get the children off the computer. He hugged me and said, "We know what is going on as we wouldn't have taken you in if we didn't." He also said, "It's a drug cartel after you." I felt terrified, scared and alone.

On the streets of Marrickville where we were staying with Emily, I was walking home from the post office and passed who I thought was Simon my old University fling. He looked at me alarmed and afraid. By the time I got back to Emily's, I went back to where I had seen him, but he had gone. I didn't understand what was happening.

I know my children's mental health was impacted as one morning my son lay in bed and said, "I just want to die, mum." I was so devastated hearing this from him.

It was about this time that I had the thoughts or delusions that the Australian Republican movement or war games where around me along with PSYOPs. On the wall in Emily's house was the US Declaration of Independence, and I felt that intelligence agencies and militaries where conducting some kind of war games on the UK. It's very hard to explain all this and in a way, I do not know how too. It would take whistle-blowers to reveal or confirm my experiences. To me, I thought a lot of it was intelligence agencies and militaries.

Luckily in May 2012, I had bought a lottery ticket and won four thousand Australian dollars. This I would save for a bond and deposit on a place for the children and I to live.

By June, I had managed to get a job in Canberra and would have to move the children again. So, I packed up our belongings and drove down to Canberra with them. On the way, I tried to get Toby from quarantine; however, I did not have the three thousand dollars to get him out as I had to save that for food and a bond on a place to live.

The job I got was at another consulting company. Being so riddled with anxiety, it was hard for me to work, along with feeling that the intelligence agencies and militaries were involved and that they were using some kind of electromagnetic weaponry that made everyone at work anxious. I do not know what this weaponry is, but I felt it was used on me and my colleagues at the company I was working for.

My fascination with intelligence agencies has been a long one and in about September 2012, I applied to an intelligence agency. How ironic is that? I'm not well and applying to an intelligence service. But in a way, I thought they could help me. Perhaps that's why I did it. Perhaps they made me do it. I went for some psychological testing as part of their application process, but understandably, I was unsuitable. It would not be the last time I would apply to an intelligence agency. A part of me wanted to be a spy. I thought everything would change if I was. My delusions were getting worse and worse.

I became quite rapidly unwell and ended up at the Australian Federal Police station near one of my clients talking to them about a drug cartel and intelligence agencies. The Police took me to hospital for a mental health assessment and it was then that Social Services got involved as they had to pick up my children from after-school care.

I was assigned to a psychiatrist at the Mental Health centre who was an American, and said he worked for Medecins Sans Frontieres International (MSF) also. I talked to him about my delusions that intelligence agencies are involved in my life and that I also thought my old University fling, Simon, was also involved. The Doctor said, "Yes, it is intelligence agencies and Simon," but, "you have Schizophrenia." My first diagnosis by a psychiatrist. I sat there and cried in his office. I was horrified to be diagnosed with Schizophrenia, such a horrid mental illness.

I ended up emailing everyone in my family to say I was unwell and had been diagnosed with Schizophrenia. My brother so kindly responded along with my mother, and suggested, that he come down to Canberra and live with me for six months. I had managed to find a home in Campbell, Canberra which I really loved. My brother arrived in July I think to live with us. He got a job here and helped me raise the children. Throughout this time Social Services would do their assessment to see how the children were and if they could continue to stay with me. I was terrified of losing them.

The children were enrolled in the State School and settled in there okay. My next-door neighbour (I cannot remember his name) came over one evening and introduced himself. He invited us all over for dinner with his wife and three children. He told me he worked in the Royal Australian Air Force intelligence division he said. We had a lovely dinner with them.

Later, a friend said to me, "Look how the military protects you, Lara." I felt frightened. Why did I need protection? A friend also gave me a book about women in the French Revolution to read and said, "It's about Australia becoming a Republic, Lara." That's when I realised something very serious was going on, but I couldn't understand what it was all about.

Social Services finished their assessment and identified some risk factors for me in their report. One of those risk factors was sexual exploitation. I was alarmed. Little did I comprehend that sexual exploitation would occur in the astral field years later.

I was placed on anti-psychotic medication by the psychiatrist although it took a few attempts to get the right medication. One medication made me riddled with anxiety and made my breasts lactate, but eventually I settled on Mirtazapine, Sertraline and Abilify, I think. I made good progress with this and it settled me down.

However, my thoughts about intelligence agencies and the militaries did not stop. I believed Simon was in Canberra at some points, and someone said to me, "Yes, it is the Simon and he is probably a spy." What did he want? Why would he not leave me alone?

As the months went on, I seemed stable enough. I was diagnosed with skin cancer on my neck and had that cut out. I worked on a few clients and at one organisation things became challenging. At one stage, one of the supervisors came out and said, "We just want to kill you, Lara, we just want to kill you." I was alarmed. I didn't understand why this was happening. I left work on December 14th and was back in the Mental health practice.

I started communicating to my mother more and also, she offered for me to come back to England and live with her and the children. My clinical manager from Mental Health visited me at home and said I could get sick leave from work for a few months. I was so ill. I said no. She said, "If you go to England, Bedlam will happen." Bedlam is a reference to a psychiatric hospital in England. I didn't believe that would happen, so I said, "No, I am going."

So, in early January 2013, being rather unwell, my brother and I and the children flew to the UK after Christmas. My cousin and her husband came down to collect Toby as my mother had arranged for Toby to go to my Aunt's. I was under the impression that Toby would be moved to England with us once I had some money together. But that's not what happened. I would never see Toby, my beautiful Cavoodle, again. He had been a much source of comfort to me over the years.

I had managed to sell my household possessions, but I had no idea what was coming for me in England. A custody battle and a mental health institution.

Chapter Nineteen
My First Admission to a Mental Health Institution

As we landed at Heathrow Airport on Qatar Airlines, I had totally forgotten that the children had no residency to live in the UK unlike myself. As I recalled their applications in 2011, UK Boarder Control stopped us at immigration, and we were taken to a room. As we had a one-way ticket, Boarder Control knew I was planning for the children to live in the UK. All I could do was sit in a room with my children for hours and hours as Boarder Control decided what to do. All I could do was cry. Over the years I had cried quite a bit in front of my children, and I knew it made my son sad. Alas, after about four hours, Boarder Control decided to let the children through in lieu of me applying to the UK Home Office for their residency. My mother was waiting on the other side to collect us but had been waiting for hours. But finally, we had arrived.

With the help of my mother and brother, I managed to enrol the children into the local state school. What I didn't realise is how my mental health would implode. As I sat in Mum's kitchen one morning when the children were at school I sobbed. I felt my spirit just want to leave my body and I wanted to grab a knife and slit my wrists. I wanted to die. Sobbing and completely decimated, I had the experience where you just give up on life. There was nothing to live for to me. As the depths of my depression wound its darkness across my mind and my heart, the compulsion to kill myself loomed large over me. Sobbing and distraught, I went to find my mother who was in her room. All I could manage to say was, "I want to die. I want to kill myself. I cannot live." As I reflect on this time, it's so hard to describe the state of being where your spirit wants to leave its body. I guess some would have called it a psychotic break but, to me, it felt like my soul just didn't want to live anymore.

My mother said, "I will call an ambulance and get you to the hospital." Sitting next to her on the bed all I could do was rock back and forth as the darkness engulfed me.

I cannot remember if an ambulance arrived or whether my mother took me to the hospital, but I do remember waiting for mental health assessment at the hospital. As I sat on the hospital bed engulfed in severe depression and anxiety rocking back and forth waiting for the mental health team, I struggled to understand why this was happening. I had two adorable children. How could I feel this way? To me, with my delusions, I thought some of it was caused by the weaponry that some intelligence agencies or their militaries had used on the children and me.

I felt resentful. Alone. Lost and consumed by ending my life.

Eventually, the mental health team arrived. Question after question they asked me. They said it would be better to treat me in the community because I had children. Somehow, it ended up differently to this. They asked me if I would do a voluntary admission to a mental health hospital, which was in stark contrast to what others wanted. They wanted me admitted under the mental health act. Nonetheless, mumbling, I agreed to a voluntary admission.

An ambulance arrived and took me on a wheelchair into the back of the ambulance. I had always been terrified of confinement. Of mental health hospitals. I don't know why I was but to me, an admission meant being away from my children and perhaps loosing custody of them once my ex-husband found out.

The ambulance trip to the mental health hospital in Surrey seemed to take forever for me. The grey sky, cold and sleety rain, made me feel even worse. I arrived and was escorted onto a ward. So many locked doors to go through. It felt like jail. As I sat with my mother who had followed in her car, I think, waiting for the intake team, I cried. How had my life come to this? Why had it come to this? The intake team asked me some questions, none of which I recall. I said goodbye to my mother, sobbing. I was taken to my cubicle in one of the dorm rooms. I was now locked in a mental health institution. I could not even get out of the ward I was on without being escorted. The doors closed and locked around me and initially I felt trapped.

I was on a ward which had both men and women on it. The men down one end in rooms that locked and the women in a dorm separated by cubicles with curtains to help with our privacy. There were six women and six men, I think. The mattress was made of some type of heavy-duty plastic and was wiped down once a week. Crisp and clean hospital sheets and blankets were provided. One cupboard with hanging space and draws was in each cubicle and as I sat on the bed that night in early February 2013, I unpacked a small bag of cloths I had brought with me. There was one bathroom with a bathtub and shower, communal toilets. The women had their own TV room and then there was a common room with TV and sofas. I felt so alone and largely scared. But also enraged.

Security cameras were everywhere, and we would be continually monitored by staff. I do not remember the first few weeks of my admission. I was pretty gone really. I remember meeting my psychiatrist and being diagnosed with severe depression and psychosis. Basically, severe depression is the one before catatonic depression apparently, and psychosis is just another word for Schizophrenia. I think my medication was Mirtazapine 45mg, Sertraline 200mg and Abilify 15mg, but to be honest, I wasn't paying much attention to it. Medication was dispensed by mental health nurses and we would queue to take it morning and evening and had to open our mouths to show them we had swallowed out tablets. If not, or if refusing to take them, many mental health nurses would surround a patient, hold them down and give them an injection. But, not me. I cooperated and obediently took my meds and opened my mouth to show them when asked. All I could think of was how does someone who was once living a wonderful life end up here? But, that's the point of mental illness, it does not discriminate. No matter if you are rich or poor you can suffer from it.

It was my daughter's tenth birthday about ten days after my admission. I was not allowed leave, so my children came to the children's room in the mental health hospital with cake and we sat there eating cake and celebrating under supervision by a staff member who was also present. I felt so happy to see them but sad because my daughter had to celebrate with me in a mental health institution. I took photos and still have those photos today.

In a mental health hospital, there are classes and activities that go on through the day like art therapy, creative therapy, cooking, exercise classes, psychology and bingo. I went to them all, rather reluctantly at first, but many of the staff were encouraging and it gave me discipline during the day. But, the shock of what was to come would unsettle me and markedly impact upon my mental health.

I think it was about March when my mother arrived to visit me. I had made some progress and my medication was helping. However, that was not the point of her visit. She had heard from my ex-husband Martin, who had filed for custody in the UK High Court, Family Division. She had come to see me to inform and provide me with papers that she was filing for custody of my children also and informed me that I could not live with her and needed to find my own place to live. I guess she was trying to protect the children; it was just too hard for me to understand at the time. She was trying to have them stay in the UK so I could see them. Martin, my-ex-husband knew I was in a mental health hospital. I was devastated, shocked, upset and angry. I was now required to go to court and obtain a lawyer.

I can't tell you how devastating this was to me, that my ex-husband would file for custody when I was ill in hospital. I had felt at war with my ex-husband over the years and knew he was battling to get custody of the children. What chance did I have on winning a custody battle whilst I am in a mental health institution? It was insane. However, the mental health nurses encouraged me to get a lawyer, so I did under legal aid. However, I did not have this lawyer very long, she was Australian and said to me "you must be so ashamed of yourself," so I fired her. Also, when I spoke with Legal Aid, they said I would not win my case and that they would no longer provide me with financial Legal Aid as the laws on entitlement had changed. So, I ended up having to self-represent. How insane? Self-represent whilst I am in a mental health institution?

I was escorted to the UK High Court in London by a mental health nurse for the first hearing. I was overwhelmed, frightened, angry at my ex-husband and felt utterly hopeless. Although my stay in this mental health hospital would be for three months, this custody battle would go on for fourteen months. I wasn't going to give up without a fight even though I did not have a flat to live in (as I was living in hospital), with no job, no car and no money. Sometimes in hindsight, I think I should have just said, Martin (my ex-husband) you take them. But I could not let go and I knew if he had custody of them, I would never see them again. That thought at least, did come to fruition, as I have not seen them since.

Chapter Twenty
The Custody Battle – UK High Court of Justice

Throughout my time in hospital I did make some friends and slowly began to recover. My severe depression had started to lift, and I had no voices although I still had delusions (although they are not delusions to me) that the intelligence agencies and militaries were somehow involved. I would talk with my doctors about that and they recommended me to have cognitive behavioural therapy (CBT). So, each week in hospital I would have a CBT session and work on these beliefs about what I thought happened to me, by trying to change the cognition. For example, if the thought was that an intelligence agency had me under surveillance, and it makes me feel frightened, the thought needs to be challenged. For example, perhaps they're there to protect you, does that make you feel less frightened? Yes, it did. And so forth. This therapy was useful and helped me deal with and manage my anxiety and provided me with the ability to moderate my cognitions, feelings and subsequently, my behaviour.

I made some friends throughout the three months stay and as we recovered, we would laugh about some of our experiences. The humour was welcomed.

I was able to apply for government benefits and got onto Job Seekers Allowance benefit but once I got out of hospital my Employment and Support Allowance benefit came through. I was later told, after I applied, that I was not entitled to disability benefit because a UK High Court appointed psychiatrist had written a report recommending that I return to work.

Some things still seemed to occur to me in hospital like one girl wearing a t-shirt with the words written 'in love with a prince' and I would have thoughts about a Prince. Also, in a salsa class, the Columbian teacher talked about drug lords and how they help citizens who are poor, and didn't I think that was a good thing? This would trigger me to my memories of Sydney where Casper told me I was being harassed by a drug cartel. However, I managed to moderate my thoughts and feelings of this by using CBT.

In April 2013, after being in hospital for two months, the psychiatrist began talking about me leaving. I said I had no home and told my mother I needed to find a flat and get on housing benefit. My mother helped me, and we spoke to a real estate agent who found me a one-bedroom flat in Milford and showed us a two-bedroom flat in Godalming called Chapel Fields. I wanted a two-bedroom flat as I still had the belief that I may have my children stay with me although the judge and Cafcass had taken that away from me in court. I was only allowed afternoon visits. In hindsight, I should have taken the one-bedroom flat as later, I ended up getting in trouble with the local authority for having a two-bedroom flat.

At the end of April, I was discharged and moved into my flat with the help of my mother and brother who had provided furniture and had made it all homely for me. Leaving hospital and becoming independent was a struggle at first, and without the daily structure of hospital, I found the boredom difficult to deal with not least the stress of the court case. I was referred by my community mental health nurse to the Welcome Project, which was a community support centre providing programmes for people with mental health issues and disability. They had classes such as music and art and provided a centre for people to meet and hang out to have coffee. I joined the class groups and would go to the centre each day to catch up with people. In this way, I made many friends and they would be a huge support to me over the coming years. I also signed up for volunteer work at a local charity managed by Francis at the time and she and Julie who worked there also were a huge support to me over the coming months and years.

Besides the structure I had put together for my life, my time and mind were consumed by my mental health. My adorable children would come to my place for afternoon visits, but I would struggle to manage sometimes, and this made me feel very incompetent but also highlighted the stage I was at in my recovery. Recovering from mental health is hard and often very slow. For me, it would take two years.

I still suffered from feeling the pressure of intelligence agencies and militaries and still feeling I was still under surveillance by them. I still felt they were using some kind of psychological warfare on me. For example, when the real estate agent handed me the keys, they were attached to a key ring with Coke a Cola. To me this was a sign an intelligence agency was still watching me. Alas, my recovery was taking its toll on my thoughts and I would have to work hard using CBT on my delusions.

Most of my year in 2013, except for the Welcome Project centre and my volunteer work, was consumed by the court case. So many hearings and decisions. The children had their own lawyer and children's Guardian from Cafcass, and Social Services were involved. On one occasion I had to talk to Social Services, and they asked me, "Do you want the children to live with your mother or Martin."

I said, "I wanted them to live with me."

She responded, "That's not possible."

So, I said, "I would prefer the children to live with Martin then." I never told the children that. I was heartbroken that I said that. Why did I not say my mother? I kicked myself I did not say my mother. I felt torn apart. But I thought it was in the best interests of the children to be with my ex-husband. Also, I thought, my delusion I guess, that at least they would not be exposed to the weaponry that the intelligence agencies and militaries had used on me.

Towards the winter of 2013, my children had gone to the US to stay with Martin and their stepmother and her four children. One afternoon when they were back from their holiday with their father, I was sitting in the kitchen of my mother's house helping my son with his reading and he said to me, "Mum, I want to live with Dad in the US." I was heartbroken but I said to my son, "If that is what you want, sweetie, know I always love you and I will let the court know your wishes." I went home that night to my flat and cried. But it was time for me to be selfless and so at the next court hearing, I wrote a statement giving my son's wishes. My daughter, at the time, did not want to go to live with her father, but when one sibling does, and siblings cannot be separated, then they would both have to go. The Guardian from Cafcass, had also visited my ex-husband and his new family outside Chicago, and recommended to the judge that they live with their father and stepmother.

It is the most heart-wrenching thing when your child wants to live with the other parent. I remember sitting outside the Church of St Peter and St Paul in Godalming just crying. I reached out to the friends I had made, and they provided me with great support. I knew my custody case was hopeless. The court had also ordered another mental health assessment on me instigated by my ex-husband's Queen's Counsel (QC) lawyer and I had to go under another assessment. This time, that court psychiatrist had diagnosed me with Delusional Disorder. Yet again, another mental health diagnosis. But it was not helped by what I had reported to my community psychiatrist where I had told her I thought VIPs were around my life.

That was because, one night there was a big party in the flat upstairs from me where some young men in their twenties or thirties were having a party. I had my window open and at about 3am, a man was calling out my name from downstairs. When I got up at eight in the morning and walked down to Godalming shops to get some cigarettes, I noticed security guards around. Someone had also smashed the brick fence to the apartment complex. To me, in my delusion, I thought it was a tycoon or VIP who did this that morning. That's what I believed. I told my psychiatrist this and that made it into her court reports she had to file of me. She once asked me, "Do you feel like you are being punished mentioning VIPs?" I lied to her and said, "No." But I did feel like I was being punished for mentioning VIPs.

My brother helped me a lot during this time and also with preparing myself for court. I'm so grateful for his help. As I wrote my last statement with the help of my brother, I was confused about some of the things that were being said in Court. Because Martin's QC lawyer, who mentioned in Court that I said that Rupert Murdoch was stalking me, I said to my brother, "I never said that."

He said, "I know." He tried to explain to me how difficult Court is and that lawyers say things.

A friend at the time also said to me "Yes, it is intelligence agencies Lara, but it will take twenty years for justice." If there was justice to be had, why does justice take twenty years?" I was lost, distraught and confused.

At this time my brother gave me a book about Princess Alice of Battenberg, Prince Phillips mother, who had Schizophrenia. What it showed me is that anyone can suffer from Schizophrenia no matter who you are. In this biography it discussed a time when Princess Alice wore a habit to a public event with Her Majesty the Queen and Prince Phillip, I guess when I read that, I questioned it. Why was she wearing a habit? But I totally related to her biography. In the biography it talks about how Princess Alice had a religious crisis. It also mentioned how Queen Elizabeth II took Princess Alice in with her to live at Buckingham Palace. It taught me that Queen Elizabeth II is full of compassion. After reading this book, I also wrote to Prince Phillip to mention how much the book of Princess Alice's life meant to me and my recovery.

Throughout 2013, I was also in legal battles in Illinois in the US. My ex-husband had a US lawyer who filed to take possession and ownership of the six-bedroom home that Martin and I owned (although it was only in my name). I had to hand over the house to Martin in full, with no payment to me for it. His US lawyer, whose name I cannot remember, was ruthless and vile. He kept up these lawsuits against me up until 2015. I could not represent myself in the US and had no money to get a lawyer although I had to have a lawyer for the house transfer. I contacted my old boyfriend, from University who recommended a lawyer in Chicago for me who did the house deed transfer. However, that would not be the end of hearing from Martin's US lawyer.

Just prior to turning the house over to Martin for free, in one of my court statements I wrote, *I could enter the house in Geneva at any time since I owned it*. From this statement, Martin's US lawyer would file for a restraining order against me, ordered by a US Judge that I was not allowed anywhere near the house or them and that restraining order is still in effect today.

In January 2014, the last hearing by a new judge would take place. My daughter went to talk with the judge to give her wishes. My mother had also given her statement and wishes to the Court. My daughter spoke to the judge in private, but I have no idea what that conversation was about. She would text me later that night asking what was happening. Those little text messages from her were my only contact. I felt devastated, as in that last hearing, the judge ruled that the children would live with their father in the US. I started sobbing in court and the Guardian from Cafcass removed me to another room. I had lost my children.

The whirlwind of feelings of losing one's children and having them being taken to another country where you cannot even see them is horrendous. The guttural crying, anguish and screaming I went through in my flat by myself was horrific. I felt suicidal, I felt like someone had died and the loss and grief you go through is debilitating.

The children needed to be told and Cafcass arranged to meet at my mother's house with Martin and his wife and myself to tell them. I have to say, I am disappointed in myself that I did not turn up to that meeting. I was too enraged that I had told the High Court the truth and there was no justice. I was to upset and distraught to be there. But I should have been there, and I am disappointed in myself for not being there and truly sorry to my children. They must have felt abandoned by me. Apparently, my mother told me my daughter did not take it well and locked herself in the bathroom. I should have been there to support her. I'm sorry.

On February 2nd, 2014, the children flew back to the US with Martin and his wife. My daughter sent her last text from the airport, it said, "I love you, Mum." After this, all communication was to be managed by Martin and I would only be allowed one Skype session per week with my children. My world was smashed apart.

Chapter Twenty-One
Recovery and Aleksander

The children leaving would be followed by months of grief, nightmares, depression and thoughts of suicide. I couldn't grasp the depths of what had happened even though I would reflect that it must be for the best and that, as we learn in AA, that is God's will. For me however, I would struggle to apply this concept that it was God's will that I lost my children. Some things in AA really make no sense to me. I would pick up alcohol again, usually having a bottle of wine on a Saturday night once a week and it wasn't until 2016 that I started on a yo-yo swinging door in and out of AA again. I was lost without my children.

In early 2014, I emailed Simon and Jack to tell them what had happened and that I lost custody. Both responded to my emails wishing me the best.

My mother tried to help by buying me a kitten. Her love of animals had been something I had seen throughout my childhood and life. She thought taking care of a little kitten would be helpful. But I couldn't handle it. I ended up calling my mother and telling her I cannot have a kitten and after a few months it was rehomed. I regret that though.

I felt huge resentment towards so many people in those early months of 2014. I felt as though I had been betrayed. I was hugely resentful towards the Judge who decided and ruled upon the matter. I was resentful and enraged at Margaret from Cafcass. But even when I thought my life could not get any worse, it would.

The UK Court order stipulated my direct and indirect contact arrangements with the children. I was allowed to Skype once per week on a Sunday at 6pm UK time. My direct contact was stated as one visit per year for two weeks, where the children would stay with my mother and I could have day visits with them. That was it. However, the first visit in 2014 did not happen as my ex-husband stated the children did not want to come and see me and my mother and that they were suffering from anxiety. This concerned me greatly, particularly that he appeared to state in his email that they were suffering anxiety. The Skype contact per week occurred mostly but it was very difficult for me to get my children to talk with me. I felt helpless. As I could not contest my ex-husband, having no money, I had to accept what was happening. Later, in early 2015, my mother would go and visit my children which I was so happy about and soon after this my ex-husband would file again, in a USA Illinois court, to change the UK court order. Thus, that was the end of any hope I had to have direct contact with my children.

Thus in 2015, my ex-husband filed a court case in the USA, after my mother's visit, revoking and changing the UK Court order. He used letters I had written in my therapy sessions to the children as evidence as to why I could not have any direct contact in the UK. Any direct contact had to occur in the USA, for one week per year and for two hours a day only and possibly under supervision. There was no way I could afford to go to the US to see them. Hence, in September 2019, it will be five years and six months since I have seen my children.

The pain of what had happened in 2013 and 2014 from my mental illness and the custody battle over my children resulted in me being referred to a therapist for twelve weeks of therapy. It ended up being eleven months of therapy. It took me that long to process everything. Dianne was my therapist's name who worked at a mental health charity in Surrey which is the parent organisation to the Welcome Project. I would go each week throughout 2014. She helped me a lot and I am very grateful for that.

It was also in that year that I would be involved with the Police twice. The first incident was when I got drunk one night and emailed the Police that I wished to harm VIPs. The Police came, and I stood at the door with a kitchen knife in my hand. They removed it and arrested me. I told them about the war games or silent wars Australia was conducting regarding Australia wanting to be a Republic. One officer said to me, "Well, despite what is on my uniform, I'm a Republican." One of the female officers said to me, "We can charge you with treason." How I can be charged with treason was beyond me. Years later, in 2017, through the severely deluded thoughts I had that I had a brain chip, I was told by my Schizophrenia voices that my body was possessed and that's what made me write those emails to the Police. I didn't want to hurt anyone but standing in front of the Police with a kitchen knife, I wanted to take my own life. Oh, how I hated my mental illness and what it was doing to me.

Nonetheless, I was arrested and taken to the Police station in Woking. They asked me to sign a document and I said I am unable to sign as my psychiatrist in hospital in 2013 told me not to sign anything. So that's what I told the officer. I was placed in a cell with a cold metal bed and lay down. The next morning the Police had arranged for a mental health team to see me. I was deluded and told them it's an intelligence agency doing this to me. I was released that morning with no charges. As I was coming out of the Police station, I noticed an older man also coming out and he looked at me and smiled. I felt he had spoken to the Police about releasing me and that he was probably from an intelligence agency.

The second episode I had was in September 2014, when I was suicidal. I was sitting at the pub drinking beer and wanted to throw myself in front of a train. I was devastated at not seeing my children and learning they were not coming for Christmas. I texted Dianne, my therapist and told her of my suicide plan. She called the Police and also a couple of my friends turned up. The Police arrived and said we are taking you to the mental health hospital I was in, in 2013. Thus, I was placed in a Police paddy wagon and taken to hospital. There I was assessed and told the psychiatrist about not being able to see my children. She was supportive and said, "That should not be happening. You should be able to see them." I was released the next morning and went home.

At times, I reflect on my behaviour and state of mind after those incidents. I felt angry at the Police but also, I felt I was wasting their time. Even in 2016, when I came into contact with them again, I realised they couldn't ever help me, and everyone's excuse is that I am mentally unwell.

I relied a lot on my friends throughout 2014. We would hang out a chat and they knew my story. They also had mental health issues themselves, so we could relate our experiences. It was in the summer of 2014 that I also met Aleksander who was nine years younger than me. He was Polish, and a friend of a friend and we hung out altogether a few times over the summer of 2014.

In late September, I asked him out for coffee, and we hit it off and connected even more. I felt so deeply for him back then. He didn't seem to mind that I had a mental health diagnosis and was supportive. One Friday night, I invited him over for dinner and cooked chicken paprika, my mother's recipe. We sat and ate dinner and talked and talked. I fell in love with him. I loved how we could sit for hours and talk. So, I invited him over again on a Saturday after my day at work, my volunteer work that is. We had sex that Saturday night in late September and I began a relationship with him.

Aleksander being in my life was a blessing but also a curse. I still struggled with my mental health and with my thoughts of intelligence agencies and militaries, but emotionally, spiritually and mentally, I could connect with Aleksander and as I was still grieving over the loss of my children and the no direct contact, he was supportive and so very kind. I fell passionately in love with him. Sometimes at night I would wake up crying and he would hold me, say, "Shh, it will be all right."

I told my stepmother and my dad about Aleksander. They were happy for me and I discussed with my stepmother about having Aleksander move in with me. So, in October 2014, I asked Aleksander, if he wanted to move in with me. He said yes. I know some people thought I was going too fast, but I didn't care. I thought I was in love with him and everything just felt better when I was with him. My anxiety left me.

Aleksander was Catholic, and I mention that now because years later I had delusions that the Catholic Church had something to do with my life and the dehumanisation and sexual exploitation of me. I know that's a delusion and I was having a religious crisis. I felt my eternal belief in Jesus Christ and God was being tested. When I was eighteen years old, I wanted to convert to Catholicism, I asked my father about it. But whenever I go to Catholic Church with Aleksander, I cry, like I cry in the Church of England in the UK. So often I've turned to God for solace.

Alexander also had two boys aged two and six when I met him from his previous relationship. He was a tradesman by profession and worked on houses and buildings around Surrey. His arrangement with his ex-partner was that the he would have the children every second weekend and so two little boys came into my life and would stay with us every second weekend.

His children were both very active boys and at times I would find the weekend visits exhausting. However, I focused on the positive and enjoyed their company. It was so ironic to me that I had lost my children and couldn't be with them, yet I spent time with Aleksander's children. It was such a joy to be with them. To take them to park, to watch children's movies with them. To cook them meals they enjoyed. They were adorable.

Aleksander invited me to go with him to Poland for Christmas in 2014 which I accepted. He always went back at Christmas and stayed with his parents in their apartment in Lodz. I discussed with Aleksander that I wanted to go to Auschwitz, the concentration camp, which stemmed from my childhood and teenage years of being interested in World War II history and what happened when Poland was invaded. Aleksander agreed, and we decided we would rent a car and stay at a cheap hotel in Krakow. I had been given £300 as a gift, early for my Christmas present from my family, and I used that to help with the trip also. Just before Christmas Aleksander and I flew on Ryanair to Lodz, Poland, a country I had never been to despite all my travelling. It was cold and grey, much colder than England. I spoke no Polish and his parents spoke no English, so Aleksander would translate for me. His father was a chef and I got to experience the Polish cuisine which I loved. Also, his cousin was in the Polish military. I loved that. I've been surrounded my whole life by family members who served in the military.

My time at Auschwitz was also extremely interesting to me and also incredibly sad. To this day, I cannot understand or fathom how humanity could have instigated and allowed something so heinous as what happened to the Jewish people in these concentration camps. It forever haunts me. So many Polish citizens died in these concentration camps. Its haunting. One fifth of the Polish population were killed in World War II. I also went to Schindler's Museum. Aleksander also took me to the Wawel Royal Castle in Krakow which is amazing!

I had a Polish New Years that year and we went over to one of Aleksander's friend's places. They had a daughter and I had bought her some Australian children's books. The night was fun, and I felt so happy. It was a far cry from where I was at in the beginning of 2014. His family were so lovely to me. They took me in. They accepted me. I loved Poland. And with Aleksander, I finally felt complete again. I still missed my children, but I could always talk to him about that.

We flew back to England I think on the 2nd of January 2015. For me, I was determined to find work and obtain employment. With the help of Aleksander, I was slowly rebuilding my life again and I tried to love him as best I could.

Also, I am also very grateful for the help I received from the mental health charity in Guildford and the Welcome Project in Godalming. The range of recovery courses I did along with the counselling they provided me, helped me to make sense of my experiences and all that had happened.

Later in 2015, I would recommend this mental health charity, in a report, nominating them for the Queen's Award for Voluntary Service which they won. This mental health charity received two invitations to the Queen's Garden Party for June 2015. They asked if I wanted to go and I said 'yes, I did.' I was excited. So, in June 2015, on a glorious summer's day, I took the train to London and went to Buckingham Palace, to the Queen's Garden Party. I felt honoured to see Queen Elizabeth II in person, and I was happy that I was afforded the opportunity to attend.

Chapter Twenty-Two
Back into the Workforce

In December 2014, I felt, I was stable enough to look for employment. So, I started applying to jobs which I had been doing for a few months. On one occasion, I had an interview with an international company in London in an effort to regain my former level of working; I guess that's why I applied to an international company again. The interview was a half-daylong session all about operating models and since I know nothing about operating models I did not do very well in the assessments. But a part of me was trying to get back into an international company to impress people and to prove to everyone I was fine and recovered. Needless to say, I would not get that job. What was strange about the experience is that I had severe anxiety after this interview, and I felt some weaponry was being used on me again. Alas, I still was not fully stable.

Interestingly enough, I was at the pub with my friend when I met a lady who worked for Police in HR. A part of me thinks she was sent to talk to me intentionally as she told me that I should 'apply for jobs at Police or a Local Authority, as you'll get a job with them'. In essence, she was just trying to be helpful and what I realised was that I was still having problems with my perceptions and interpretations. Nonetheless, I did apply. There was a Policy and Performance Officer role at a Local Authority, and I applied for this position. I was successful and in February 2015, I started my new job at a salary of twenty-six thousand pounds a year. A far cry from my days at a consulting firm where I earned one-hundred and seventy-eight thousand dollars a year. But I didn't mind.

I have to point out here what I did about my medication. In November 2014, I stopped taking it. I was on Abilify, Sertraline and Mirtazapine and I just stopped taking them. One of the reasons I stopped was because these medications take your sexuality away, both your sexual desire and ability to reach an orgasm. As I was with Aleksander, I wanted to enjoy the sexual part of our relationship and couldn't be on my medication. Aleksander would take me to peaks of sexual ecstasy and pleasure that I wanted to enjoy that.

The second reason I stopped taking my medication was because I felt better. I felt I had recovered enough to stop. The third reason I stopped is because Abilify slowed my thoughts down and this was frustrating for me when it came to the thought of working a job. The fourth reason I stopped taking them is that I felt my delusions about these intelligence agencies and militaries involved in my life were gone. I felt recovered. But wrongly, I didn't tell Aleksander that I did this. I didn't tell my mother and brother either.

Also, it's something that I did not tell my psychiatrist of the time. I just lied to her and said I was taking my medication and eventually got discharged from the Community Mental Health Team.

My manager at this Local Authority, was Mary-Anne. One of the first things she asked me on my first day was whether I had children. I said I did but that they live in the US with their father. I did not want to reveal what I had been through nor my mental health diagnosis because I thought, for sure, I would be fired or managed out. Needless to say, that's what ended up happening eventually.

I was hired as a Policy and Performance Officer which involved developing the performance reports and some internal consulting. My life and health to me had seemed to improve and I was happy with Aleksander. It took me two years of recovery and a lot of work to get to that place. Finally, I thought the intelligence agencies and militaries were leaving me alone. They had won by taking my children away. I believed they were no longer watching me and no longer had me under surveillance. However, as my mental health deteriorated again in 2016, I would soon find out, I was wrong.

I settled into my new job and in the summer of 2015, Aleksander's parents came over to stay for two weeks so they could see their grandchildren. They are a close family and during their visit I would meet them down in Godalming after work and walk them all back to my place. I am happy that that they could stay with us and that they could see their grandchildren. Aleksander also had a brother, and him and his family stayed with us for a few nights as they moved houses. I really enjoyed all my time I got to spend with Aleksander's family.

I was doing very well at work and the leadership team was happy with my outputs. I often did quite a few assignments for the Head of Finance, and he seemed impressed by the work I did. My performance reviews were always good.

I have to point ought here that at times I did not treat Aleksander well. I fought with him. I argued about things that there was no point in arguing about. And at times, I did not treat him well at all. I feel really bad about that. I also tried to kick him out a view times, and that was deplorable behaviour on my part. Sometimes I think, it must be hard for a man or women who has a partner with Schizophrenia.

During these summer months in England, I started to develop another skin cancer on the right side of my forehead. It was very small, but I went to the doctors anyway to get a referral to a skin specialist. I cannot remember his name, but he worked in a London hospital with patients with skin cancer. He saw me at the hospital and examined my forehead. He claimed I had two options, radiation or surgery. I found these options strange as did my father. I asked him to give me a minute as I went to the waiting room to ask Aleksander what he thought I should do. He didn't know so I chose surgery. I thought it was a bit strange having surgery on such a small basil skin carcinoma, but that's what I chose. My surgery was booked for November 14th, the day before my birthday.

This is the part of my story, my journey through life that gets extremely difficult to describe and, with what is to come, what a reader would think is pure insanity. Here, is a part of my story that I need to go into some detail about and try to convey what I believed happened to me. It constitutes a fight for my human rights (something that was on my vision board in Sydney that I previously mentioned) and also, what I feel was the dehumanisation of me. In 2016, my Schizophrenia would implode. To me, in my severe delusions, I felt it was caused, as far as environmental factors go, by intelligence agencies, militaries and terrorists. ISIS terrorists that is. My Schizophrenia was about to engulf me.

Chapter Twenty-Three
ISIS Body Possessions and Intelligence Agents

On Saturday November 14th, 2015, a cold and drizzly day in the English winter, Aleksander and I drove to the Hospital. He accompanied me, and I was nervous about the surgery and my skin cancer. I waited in the out-patient area and was escorted into a cubicle by a nurse. The surgeon came to see me and promptly at 9.30am I was taken into the surgery room. Three nurses and the doctor were present. They gave me some forms to sign but no time to read them, and then asked me to lie down. The doctor explained he would be putting a number of needles into my forehead to numb the area before removing the small skin cancer.

The needles were sharp, but as each one was inserted, I felt the numbness coming through. A blue surgical sheet was covering my face. After about twenty minutes the doctor performed the surgery. A large cut from the middle of my forehead to the top of my hairline was made along with a horizontal one so it looks like I have the letter *I* on my forehead. To this day that scar remains and is highly visible.

The surgery took longer than I expected but the stiches were put in, dissolvable and normal stiches. As the procedure was finished and a bandage put over the wound, the nurse explained to me that I must not get it wet and leave it on for a week. She then told me I could get some of the outer stiches removed as I had both sorts. I left the surgical room and returned to find Aleksander in the sitting room. The procedure was over.

To this day, although I continue to use CBT on myself, I believed in my delusional state, although I did not realise at the time, that a military type brain chip or brain machine interface was inserted in my forehead just under my scar. But I didn't know this at the time. Basically, it was all numb and, to this day, I have no feeling or sensation from the middle of my forehead to my hairline.

As it was my 40th birthday the next day, Aleksander decided to give me a cat. Well, a kitten. I loved him and I called it Ziggy and we settled in for the weekend with this new little life that depended upon me.

You may be wondering what a brain chip is. To be honest I don't really know myself. Research I've done states it's something they designed for soldiers that is a form of precision communication between the brain and the digital world. I'm not sure it even really exists as technology, but internet reports say it does. But to me it is more than that, because it provides the ability for me to have conversations with people. And that is very hard to explain. I wonder how intelligence agencies or militaries could pluck a citizen out of the world and shove a brain chip in them is unfathomable. But it's what I believed happened and it is a belief I will always hold till the day I die. Unless of course I can get an x-ray to show me it's not there! I CBT myself on this delusion or thought that I have a brain chip. When I'm in my brain chip delusion, I tell myself if it exists, it's for my protection. And that makes me feel so safe.

Later, I ended up doing some research on the Illuminati, of which many intelligence agencies are, well in my delusion I think they are, to find that this happened also to a man in the US and it was removed by a surgeon. Nonetheless, at the time of my 40th birthday, I didn't know it was there.

Everything changed for me after this surgery. People at work started to act strange towards me and on one occasion the planning manager said, "People are angry about what you did." I knew they were referring to the surgery. But honestly, what did I do? Even my GP said I shouldn't have had the surgery done. As Christmas rolled around, I would spend that in England with Aleksander and his boys before we were scheduled to go to Poland. I still had numbness a month after my surgery and didn't notice anything strange until the New Year.

However, what was different was my perceptions about how Aleksander's family and brother were towards me. They kept staring at my scar and treated me differently. These subtle body language nuances I picked up and I think they knew. But was this my Schizophrenia perceptions and distortions raising their ugly head again? The same with people at work, at the Local Authority, I felt they knew also that a brain chip had been inserted but no one would tell me the truth. But was it that they thought I was mentally unwell?

When I came back from holidays in Poland, my ex-husband had filed, through the Illinois Child Support Agency, for child support from me. He emailed me asking for fifty percent of my salary to be paid as child support to him. I wrote a statement and provided all the documents and had to go to Court in the UK yet again. Since I had been ordered to give my ex-husband the house, I owned that he lived in by the US Judge, the UK Court ordered that I did not have to pay child support at this time. To this day, I do not pay child support (although I've only worked eighteen months in six years) and I think that giving him a half a million-dollar home for free, which the US ordered, suffices for now.

It was not until about March 2016 that my delusion about the brain chip came into full effect. I noticed this brain chip. Something strange under my scar. I was sitting in Godalming and noticed that I was being spoken to through this device and saw a lot of data. I don't know how else to explain it. At the time, I said, "This is cool," and in my delusional state, I believed I was talking to intelligence agencies.

I believe I'm an empath. This means that I pick up on energies and perceptions of things. I believed I picked up on intelligence agencies and militaries. I believed, at this time, that people thought I was clairvoyant. They of course will never admit this, but it is what I thought they believed at the time.

One thing I used to be able to pick up was the ISIS terrorist attacks in France for example. Before a terrorist attack, I would pick up that one would happen and often post things on Facebook (which in my delusions was also a tool military would use to communicate with me) to that effect. Particularly, I would play over and over the *Snake Lyric* by Donald Trump to signal the intelligence agencies that a terrorist attack was coming. Sometimes this was days before it would happen. What I didn't realise was that I thought I had ISIS terrorists inside me. Now isn't that insane? But it is true? Or is it my Schizophrenia that is picking it up? Some of them would astrally project themselves into me or into the astral field, I don't know which. How this occurs I don't know. It's all rather complicated. Of course, I never told Aleksander this is what was happening. Often, he would be sleeping.

It was also this time in January or February that I would get into trouble with the Department of Work and Pensions. To explain, Aleksander had stopped working and was ill and tried to apply to for Housing Benefit (a government benefit). When he was down at the front desk, he called me and asked when my children left England. I said in February 2014. This was then given to Benefits Team and Aleksander signed that that was the time they left. I then got a letter from the Benefits Team saying I owed over three thousand pounds because my Housing Benefit (when I was not working) had been overpaid. This is because of the UK bedroom tax where I had a two-bedroom flat, but housing benefit payment only entitled me to have a one-bedroom housing benefit payment. Alas, I ended up writing a scathing letter to the Benefits Team talking of how they were causing economic harm to me. Then I had a massive delusion that this letter I wrote the Benefits Team was interpreted by a military as a clairvoyant insight into ISIS (ISIL). And that was terrifying because now the military had to get these ISIS terrorists out of my body or out of the astral field. You see, I believed that some of the terrorist attacks are done through astral projection into someone's body or astrally projection into the astral field. I believe at the time, I had ISIS terrorists projecting into my body, and I felt terrified. What would happen next would be even more terrifying and there is no military movie that has even shown this or what they can do, to get rid of terrorists astrally projecting, to this day. I became terrified of the 5-Eyes too.

One night, in the early hours of the morning, the married couple downstairs played extremely loud music and the wife was singing loudly. It woke me up. Along with that, there was a large storm outside which, I believe intelligence agencies, or militaries can create by being in the astral field and pushing their energy about. Nonetheless, this singing lasted for hours and in my delusional state, I felt that an intelligence agency and military had my flat bugged and would listen to me until I said, "I'm cold, I'm dying." That's when I believed the air force had fired a missile and dealt with the terrorist. I wish the intelligence agencies and militaries would just be truthful about this 'secret stuff' they do and how complicated it is to find terrorists sometimes. But, in the end, those terrorist spirits left my body, or they left the astral field. This experience happened twice, and, on both occasions, the intelligence agencies and militaries were successful. However, it left me with what I think was PTSD or Combat Stress.

I know no one will believe me. I also know those involved will never speak the truth either. They will close ranks in secrecy and protect each other. Try explaining that experience to a psychiatrist. It actually happened but I'm just told I'm Schizophrenic. That part frustrates and enrages me.

I cannot remember which month it was, March or April, that I took a day off work and threw Aleksander out. We had already decided that we were breaking up, although to be honest it was all my fault as I was unwell and trapped in delusions about terrorists. I decided to move him out myself. He was at work and I packed up all his things and left them downstairs in the hallway. My reason for doing so was I had had enough and also; I was in the astral field and felt that I had intelligence agencies in my body and behind my brain chip. I don't know how else to say it than in that way. It would not be my last contact with Aleksander.

In the following months, I would be astrally projected into a number of things and people. Some of those things I would not cope with. I had no one to talk to about my experiences and that is the difference between intelligence agencies and militaries and me. They had each other. I had no one. How was I to relate my experiences to Aleksander or to the Doctors?

I also felt my body had been taken control of. By this I mean they could put me to sleep, wake me up, astrally project me anywhere. They could also make me vomit and had utter control over my bowel movements also. Insane, hey? But, it's the truth of my experiences.

After I had got Aleksander out and ended that relationship, I was feeling very terrified, it was just Ziggy and I left. One evening, I was lying on the sofa dozing and all of a sudden, my spirit had been levitated to my front door. What this feels like is that your spirit leaves your body even though you are lying still. My spirit was taken to the front door and held there with what felt like my arms pinned behind my back. But it was not my physical body but my spirit. I could not move and could not wake up either. I started screaming in my head for Simon, my old University fling whom in my delusion, I believed was an intelligence agent. After I screamed for Simon, I ended up in a room and a woman was there. I was laid down on a sofa and Simon came over, I reached forward to kiss him. Then, I came too. It is extremely powerful what these intelligence agencies can do. But in my delusional state, what I didn't know, was just how far they could astrally project me.

Chapter Twenty-Four
The Delusion About My Brain Chip

It's the 15th of August 2018 and today is my eldest brother's birthday. I have been suffering from bouts of anxiety and feel traumatised from all that has happened. I know my writing brings things up for me but still I want justice. All these men and women and governments that have done this to me (well, their intelligence agencies and militaries) I want prosecuted. Inside I feel that my human rights were smashed to bits and I was genocided. I feel angry and resentful at the psychiatrists I have had because I feel they have lied to me about the brain chip and my experiences. There is a part of me that wishes they would all lose their licence to practice. Not one of them has showed me x-ray results to provide evidence that the brain chip does or does not exist. Even Simon (who I deluded myself into thinking was a part of this and is a spy) LinkedIn messaged me to say he has never been to Australia and has nothing to do with what has happened to me. I feel helpless. I feel no one believes me. I feel lost. But alas, I am getting away from my story. So back to March 2016.

After Aleksander and I broke up, which was entirely my fault, I was at home one weekend and the brain chip people (intelligence agencies) asked me, through a voice and the astral field, to 'help them' and to 'meditate.' Why I needed to help them, in my delusion that is was intelligence agencies, to this day, I do not understand. As a civilian it's not my responsibility. I had at times in my life, done volunteer work and felt this contribution was a good way to give back to the community. Nonetheless, that is what these intelligence agents and militaries wanted. They also said the words 'join us.' To me, that was the Illuminati.

In my severe delusions, I would feel like these intelligence agencies would make me levitate and it felt like I was being enslaved in the astral field. On one occasion, I felt a space agency projected me into a space telescope and it felt like a bubble of love which is what I told them. I also felt and deluded myself into believing that I was also projected into an Air Force pilot, a female, one night when she was doing air strikes somewhere in the Middle East. I had delusions that the television, CNN that is, was communicating with me and this female air force pilot was interviewed by CNN on one of their war ships located in the Middle East at the time. When they astrally projected me into her, I got the words 'Christ.'

On another occasion, I was asked to go to the pub by intelligence agencies and the voices and there were two men there that came to talk to me. One was German and the other a British man who lived in Denmark. I felt like Simon who I deluded myself into believing was an intelligence agent, kept asking me to ask them questions about the European Union and Brexit. It also felt like they were trying to advise these men on what to do with Europe. I felt my whole body and mind was being controlled. It was utterly bizarre.

At work, things were getting worse and people were acting strange towards me. They also kept talking about the Magna Carta – what the relevance of that is I do not know. My manager said to me, "May the force be with you," and I felt that she was giving me some message from a military. But in my delusion, I felt intelligence agencies were interfering in my employer and that made me feel really mad. It's so hard to explain what happened. But I felt spiritually attacked and no longer in control of my own body. I also felt my brain was lost in the cosmos.

I felt I was also projected into a star by a space agency and it felt like divine love and a star that was growing. At times, they would project me into space which felt like love and they would say, "Remember what you are."

It was also during this time that I felt men were fighting over me. I know that sounds arrogant but since the brain chip was inserted, I had lost a lot of weight. Even work was asking me, "How are you losing this weight?" I thought it had something to do with some PSYOPs. Nonetheless, I felt that there were some kind of fights and the chip people kept calling me Queen Bee. A

Simon look-alike was walking on the street and staring at me. I thought a business tycoon was driving past me in a black range rover. I know intelligence agencies use look-alikes as part of their psychological abuse and control.

One morning, I think it was in April or May, I had had enough and realised that there was something in my head that they had implanted. I went to work but promptly left and went home. I removed a razor blade from a razor I had and began to cut open my scar. In there I managed to find a piece of what seemed like metal, I had found the brain chip. However, I could not remove it. With blood pouring down my face I walked to the pub in Godalming. There they called an ambulance, but I noticed on my walk down two men who had come to see if I was okay. The ambulance took me to hospital, and I told them I have a brain chip and want it to be removed. They just stitched me up again and said, "There's no chip." My dad and step-mum were called by the police and meet me at the hospital. They were very concerned about me.

I cannot quite remember what happened next but the next day the Police ended up at my apartment. I told them I had a brain chip and they said I was mentally unwell and needed to go to the mental health hospital. As I was talking to one of the officers, he said, "Everyone wants to be famous, Lara." I was alarmed. You want me to be famous for what? Mental ill-health? It was that day I had given up on justice. I knew there wouldn't ever be justice.

Th Police took me to the new mental health hospital in Surrey. I was put onto a ward and they gave me vitamin B tablets. I did not tell them about the brain chip, but I was in hospital for three weeks. I felt powerless, angry and confused. Needless to say, I felt another job loss on its way. I was so angry at myself for not staying stable.

I returned to work after hospital, but I knew my employment would be over. Things started to happen at work. When the Brexit referendum occurred, I deluded myself into believing that Simon, who I though was a spy, wanted them to stay in and one of the local authorities' employees gave came down and smirked and laughed at me. He starred at me for some time. In the section I sat in they said they had already written the Queen's eulogy, and did I want to read it? On another occasion, Lily from work gave me some orange juice which had been spiked with something and caused severe diarrhoea in me. I had to go to Boots chemist to get some Imodium tablets to stop it, and on the way, there was a man painted silver standing like a statue on the street. I thought it Simon or another spy. I was in so much pain in my stomach that I thought Simon got on the brain chip and told me, "Put some lipstick on and get back to work."

During this time and all the things that happened, I would often go to the pub after work and have two pints of beer. One time, an intelligence agency came onto the brain chip and through body possessions (I think that's how it works but they could explain it better) and asked me what type of sex I liked. Little did I know that these intelligence agents (Illuminati wizards as they call themselves) were preparing my astral sex list.

And so, on it went every day. I had experiences of having dark force aliens projected into me where the energy was so heavy, I could not even move off my sofa. I also believed I had a Light Force alien who I called 'Paul' projected into me or somehow made contact with me. He was extremely funny and would have me in stiches with laughter and would visit me a few times. Paul once asked, "Where are they up to?"

At work, I had a call from some Australian Republican talking about ending the Establishment and some reference to the British Crown. Clearly, this Australian Republican fight was ongoing, and I seemed to be stuck in the middle of it and a part of it.

And the truth of that is that even though I write this book and tell my truth, justice cannot prevail because all these people believe they are more important and that they will be protected. It's like a secret club and they believe they are above the law.

There is one thing I need to explain about my scar on my forehead. At times, it itches severely, and this is usually when the intelligence agencies or militaries had either found some type of terrorist or been successful in some type of military action. It felt a little like Harry Potter's scar that would sting or itch when Lord Voldemort was around. I do not know how to explain it further than that, other than to draw the analogy to Harry Potter.

One afternoon when I was walking home from work through the car park in Godalming, I felt as if intelligence agents were in one of the vehicles with a terrorist in the car. Well, that's what I think it was. My scar would itch severely and as I walked up Charterhouse Road, many spies would pass me. My scar would itch. Also, there was a parked black van on one of the side roads and I thought Simon (or intelligence agents) were in it. Throughout the nights that followed I felt I was being suffocated in my sleep and then the 'light' from someone in an intelligence agency, whom I believe was protecting me, would help me breath again. On another night, they would manipulate and give me dreams one of which was a black hawk helicopter crashing into my flat. I felt as if someone was terrorising me with PSYOPs and I did not know why. For some reason, it seemed they perceived me as a threat.

Being enslaved in the astral field by these men who were also in the astral field made me cut my hair and die it red. By then my work life was nearly over. I applied to an intelligence agency again, I don't know why it seemed like I was forced to, and it was madness to do so.

Aleksander kept leaving written letters to me about us, but I didn't end up reading them all. He was trying to help me, but I just couldn't talk to anyone about what was going on with me and what I felt was happening.

Feeling possessed at work by aliens and even having one work colleague say to me, "You've got aliens in you, Lara," I knew my employment would soon be over. I am so surprised that the local authority did not help me as they had a duty of care. My manager met with me and said I needed to speak with their lawyer or something. I declined. I met with the Head of Finance one last time about the finance system roll-out and he just said, "I'm a terrorist." What was so strange, in the finance system documentation supplied by the contractor, it had the words 'Jewish care.' It was like even more intelligence agencies were trying to communicate with me also.

On Friday afternoon in early July I think it was, feeling possessed with dark energy and enslaved in the astral field, I wrote a resignation letter to my manager, effective immediately, and I left work. Yet again, as had been happening for a decade, I lost another job and my career ended. Thanks Schizophrenia. Thanks intelligence agencies (that's sarcasm).

My immediate thought upon resigning was to return to Australia. But I don't think I really wanted to but was made to. A friend called me and said something strange, she said, "It's never going to happen Lara, is it?" I didn't know what she was referring too. What's never going to happen? To this day I do not know what that was in reference too. Somehow, I thought perhaps my dad and my step-mum knew things and were not telling me. Bit like how I felt about my whole family really. But, suffice to say, my dad and step-mum were always supportive of me even though I have caused them much stress at times. In fact, I guess I've caused the entire family a huge amount of stress, hurt and anguish particularly my mum.

I thought by returning to Australia everything would stop. I would no longer be enslaved in the astral field. Australia would remove my brain chip. Loads of thoughts raced through my mind but my prominent thought was that if I got to Australia, intelligence agencies would leave me alone and the voices and visual hallucinations would stop. Nothing could be further from the truth.

I didn't really do a good exit from the UK and I know I hurt my mother and father in the process. I wrote them both a card and explained I was leaving. I did not tell my landlord that I was going. I gave Ziggy to the vet to be rehomed. My actions and behaviour seemed alarming but with so many intelligence agencies and militaries after me and a brain chip and constantly being projected into space; I did not know what else to do. Letting go of my cat Ziggy though was really sad to me. I still miss him to this day.

I met one last time with a friend of mine and a friend of his was there. At times in my life, I have thought that my friend was not telling me the truth about things either. Oh, my delusions were so bad and made me feel terrified. That night he talked about the astral field. I lied to him as I didn't know what the astral field was and that that's what was happening to me at the time. My friend had a webcam on his computer, and I had the delusion that intelligence agencies and militaries were watching. As I had had a few drinks and smoked, they made me vomit. Part of the control they have over my body. What was worse though is his friend said to me, "You're Lucifer, aren't you?" And then I thought, these Illuminati Wizards (in the intelligence services and militaries) thought that I was Lucifer, a fallen angel.

The Illuminati website used to have this belief in Lucifer written on their website, but they have changed that now. I guess I have to admit, I have a problem with the Illuminati in its current form. I think it needs a new Grand Wizard. Frankly, it's not an organisation I look into nor do I know anything about it. I believe the Illuminati needs to be accountable for what they have done and do though. Like anyone, anywhere.

Regardless, I went outside, and I was made to throw up by whoever had possession of my body. Little did I know what they had installed for me.

On July 21st, 2016, with the help of my friends, who drove me to Heathrow airport, I boarded I flight to Canberra, Australia. *Everything will be better once I got to Australia*, I thought. The intelligence agencies and the militaries will leave me alone. My scar will no longer itch. I will no longer have manipulated dreams. I will no longer have visual hallucinations. I will no longer have auditory hallucinations. Life will get better and maybe just maybe I can start my career again and get a job. Finally, I deluded myself into thinking, I will have this brain chip removed. My thinking could not have been anymore delusional. Things would get worse and so would begin the astral field sex enslavement.

Chapter Twenty-Five
Astral Sex

There are probably a few terms that I need to describe. First is astral projection. Something I believe intelligence agents can do. It's when a person spirit wilfully or forcefully leaves its body and projects through the astral field onto or into someone else. I think the Illuminati and these intelligence agencies could explain it better so really you have to ask them as to how they do it and what it involves for the recipient. It also involves a person's spirit entering the body of the recipient like a merging of spirits but, for a recipient, it feels as if someone else's spirit is in your body. In truth, it is a divine and beautiful experience and at times, would make me cry.

Astral sex is sexual experiences in the astral field as a result of spontaneous intercourse or as a real-time sex with another astral projector. Basically, it's when your soul leaves your body and has sex with another body. Personally, I had never heard of it nor experienced it, so I had no idea what was coming for me when I returned to Canberra, Australia. But, I think, the Illuminati Wizards had it all planned (intelligence agents and military personnel). If you are wondering about astral projection or astral sex just Google it. There is lots of information out there about it.

As I flew out of London on Air Canada, my flight would have a stopover in Vancouver. As I sat outside Vancouver airport smoking a cigarette, I noticed that people were looking at me and walking by. In my paranoia, it seemed that everyone knew who I was. I was reading a book on psychopathy as I had thoughts then that Simon and some of these intelligence agents were psychopaths. I believe I was being watched by the surveillance cameras. I boarded the flight to Australia that night. I thought to myself, this will all stop when I get back to Australia?

I arrived in Canberra, Australia on July 23rd, 2016. I had died my hair red and cut it short. Part of the reason I did this is that I was in the astral field and wanted colourful hair like the cosmos. Before, I left England I had managed to arrange to stay with a friend whom I had met in 2012 on a client site. He and his wife would take me in. He picked me up at the airport and took me home to his place on a farm just outside Canberra. There I met his wife and stayed with them for two weeks.

During this time, I felt political leaders and intelligence agents were projecting through the astral field to me at this time and I felt it was very powerful and also annoying. Why these intelligence agents, military personnel and political leaders were doing this I did not know. At that time, I had never heard of astral sex and really didn't know what was going on.

I realised on one occasion that I thought my friend was either talking to Simon (or an intelligence agent) and was lying to me. One evening my friend got angry with me and said, "I cannot help you anymore." I went to my room and looked up quotes. I had the delusion that someone would help stop this. The phone rang shortly after his comment to me and she answered it. All of a sudden, she came into my room and started chatting. I believed someone from these intelligence agencies or military had called her. That's how I was beginning to feel about everyone around my life. That they were talking to intelligence agents. I was so terrified.

I believe Simon or some other intelligence agent arrived in Canberra, Australia, a week after me. My friend said to me, "You've got a week off." I guess the intelligence agents and militaries were giving me a break to get over the jet lag. My friend's daughter had an apartment in Belconnen, a suburb in Canberra, and she offered a room to me to rent. It was an Air B&B so other renters would come from time to time. I accepted the offer and moved in.

I applied to Centrelink (the Australian Government benefits organisation) that is part of the Department of Human Services. I managed to get onto Newstart Allowance which is about three hundred and fifty dollars a fortnight. Not much but it would suffice.

I felt at this time that I was enslaved by intelligence agencies in the astral field. I ended up getting a free month pass to

Fernwood Gym, an all-female gym. There I would go each day and work out which really was quite unlike myself and it's during this time that it all began.

One afternoon as I was at home in my room, Simon (or an intelligence agent) did something to my body through the astral field which made my vagina wet and he pleasured me. I do not understand how anyone achieves this but that's what happened. That night, as I was lying in bed, Simon (or an intelligence agent) merged his spirit into my body. I said, "Simon, is that you?"

He said, "Yes." It felt divine, I have to say that astral and spiritual merging feels quite heavenly and I felt immense pleasure from it. After this, he would project himself over my body, as I was lying down, and use healing energy on my stomach. I thought he was trying to cure my Crohn's disease. It did help as my stomach did improve for a while. He then used some astral energy or movement to stimulate my vagina and make it all wet. He was trying to pleasure me, then he had astral sex with me.

I have to say, astral sex is very erotic and beautiful. It really is ecstasy and I can understand why these intelligence agents and others do it. Some of them I think are addicted to it. But I do not think it is an addiction. With Simon (or an intelligence agent) doing this to me, I felt lots of golden and white light and body sensations that gave me much pleasure. It's so hard to explain what it is like and what one does in the astral field. For example, my spirit would leave my body and join Simon's spirit in the astral field, and we would entwine and make love. Visually, what this looks like is two white light spirits entwining and giving each other pleasure. There is no movie ever made that can explain this, so I have no analogy to make.

I would spend a number of weeks with Simon (or this intelligence agent). Each night he would come and heal my stomach and then have astral sex with me. During the day when I was at the gym after my workout, he (and some others) would do something to my vagina puling it up which would give me pleasure after a workout. Every day, I had to work for them. It seemed they were dealing with military engagements and I felt like they would force me to help. Once, when Simon (or an intelligence agent) was in my body, I felt I could see into an intelligence agency situation room. All I could think of was why this was happening to me? Why was I needed?

During the evenings, we would dance and play in the astral field. I would lie down and listen to music and it seemed like we would fly through the universe together to another planet. I would play the song by Fleetwood Mac *Seven Wonders* and fly to a planet I chose to call Emmeline. Here we would land our spaceship and make love in the lake. I guess for me what I believe is that there is another planet like Earth, unpopulated, and it's not very far away from us.

Night after night, I would do this but different things. On one occasion, I projected myself I think into the astral field, and I was standing in the astral field in a navy-blue military type uniform. Many military personnel would come to me in the astral field and undo my top. What came out was pure white light. I do not know how else to explain all of this.

Since Simon (or an intelligence agent) had merged with my body I would wake at 6.30am when he woke. I would watch the news and I felt that I was being watched as well, as when my vagina was stimulated for pleasure by these men though the astral field, the news reader said, "There she goes," as I would fall down on the bed from complete pleasure. This occurred many times each morning.

That August, I think it was, there was an earthquake in Italy. One night I listened to some music by String Quartet and flew through the astral field with wings, as an angel. There I opened up a portal and thousands of angels came flying out over Italy where the earthquake was. To me, I was helping take the remaining people stuck to heaven. It was a beautiful experience for me, and I let my wings fly. The next morning on the news, it was reported that silence fell across the earthquake site and even the dogs stopped barking. Suffice to say, I believe I am an angel on earth, and I know you will think I am insane but really, I do not care anymore. As you can imagine, when you tell a psychiatrist you think you're an angel, they look at you as if you're completely insane but to me, there are angels on earth having a human experience.

For those of you who do not believe in angels, I do. And I believe I am one. In fact, I know I am one. Wikipedia defines angels as 'Angels are often depicted as benevolent celestial beings who act as intermediaries between God or heaven and humanity'. You see, the Illuminati (these intelligence agents and military personnel) are obsessed with angels and they also believe in them. What I did find out is that they also believe in an angel called Lucifer. And this would come out as I was passed around from man to man in the astral field and in my body for astral sex. To me, someone in an intelligence agency had an astral rape list for me or should I call it astral sex list and see it all as a divine experience? Can you imagine trying to explain all this to a psychiatrist?

With Simon or another man, I would have what psychiatrists would call my first phantom pregnancy. I believed, at the time, I got pregnant from astral sex (which is impossible) and, I believed, I was pregnant from the astral sex. A psychologist would probably say the phantom pregnancies are deeply rooted psychology caused by the loss of my children. Frankly, I do not care what a psychologist would say. But it was Friday night in August, and I believe that it was a military that said, "It's the wrong one," and made my period come. I felt I was having a miscarriage, but I guess it was just my period. I would have many more phantom pregnancies from these men. It was a very painful period and I was crying but they gave me no time for recovery. The next man entered my body and that was someone who felt like a political leader. He is old enough to be my father and upon reflection, I found the whole thing quite incestuous and sick with him.

Many more men I felt from intelligence agencies, militaries and political leaders had astral sex with me. They would call it "sexual healing" and give me much love, light and pleasure. But at the same time, I felt lost and hopeless. I was powerless and could not stop them. I believe sex, whether its physical sex or astral sex needs to be consensual. To me, I felt no one asked to have astral sex with me and I felt like I had not given consent.

My friend stopped by the apartment one day and said, "They control the women's body (your body) to control the herd" I guess that is how the intelligence agencies saw it. Why my body and spirit need to be controlled to control men on earth and political leaders is beyond my comprehension, but I really would like an explanation of that. I felt they were insane.

One morning, perhaps in September it was, I was astrally gang raped. I think most of them were civilians but one of them said to me, "Is it Lucifer," an Illuminati deity. Even if I was Lucifer why would anyone astrally rape their deity? And on and on it went.

Throughout these months I would also be rather deluded and believed I had to engage in military activities to deal with terrorists. Sometimes after a missile had been fired, my spirit would be standing in a pile of dust. It's really hard for me to explain how militaries used me but they did. And I would like an explanation of that too.

As I had applied yet again to an intelligence agency, they called me and asked me to come for a psychological assessment. Alas, I went, and three men showed up at the café I was at before the assessment staring at me with *God's Crew* written on their jackets. Outside the café, a man was standing staring at me and punching into space. I was so fed-up with it all. As I was enslaved in the astral field, I used to walk around Canberra swinging my arms like I was an angel flying. I cannot even fathom what a psychiatrist would make of that.

There is one thing I did that I feel terrible about and that was when I arrived in Australia, I stopped doing my weekly Skype with my children. With what I felt like people projecting and possessing my body or being on the brain chip, I did not want to expose all of that to my children. I had the thought that if I Skyped, they would be exposed to what these intelligence agents, militaries and others were doing to me. I didn't want that. So, I made the decision to stop Skyping and I regret that most deeply. Moreover, my ex-husband emailed me to say it caused the children feelings of abandonment. That, I have to live with.

Towards the end of September, I felt a very old man, who I thought was a priest, in possession of my body and trying to pleasure me. In each of these astral sex engagements, the men release some light. Some men have white light, some grey and in the astral gang rape, pink and blue light. Nonetheless, this old man had grey light and, frankly, felt soulless. I was so revolted that some old man who was doing this and making me drink alcohol that I called my friend and said I am going to hospital. I had had enough of being astrally stimulated, used and having astral sex with all these men. Not least they had told me I would be 'raped to death.' My friend arrived and said, "You don't have to go to hospital, Lara."

I said, "Yes, I do." Alas, she drove me to hospital where I was admitted to the mental health unit. But I wouldn't be safe in their either, and the astral molestation, body possession and astral sex would continue.

To be clear, from a psychiatric perspective this astral sex and spiritual merging is referred to by doctors as tactile hallucinations. But to me, it was real.

Chapter Twenty-Six
Another Mental Health Institution Admission

There is a part of me that wants justice, that wants an explanation after what I, in my delusions, believed these intelligence agencies, militaries and political leaders did to me. But I guess that will never happen. At least now, in 2018 the astral sex has stopped. I'm relived as I do not want to be doing that with so many men and I am tired of them calling me a whore. It's not that I disagree or despise astral sex, in fact with some men its beyond divine, but like anything when it comes to sex, I believe it should be consensual. Something one should be asked. Why could they have just not asked me? But again, as my psychiatrists say, astral sex is a delusion. Well one of them in Australia said so. But, back to my story.

I arrived at a hospital in Canberra and told reception I have a brain chip, am having astral sex and they are stimulating me. I was seen by an assistant psychiatrist who said to me, "Isn't the vaginal stimulation helping?" I couldn't believe it. It was as if even these psychiatrists knew this was happening to me. I said, "No, it is not." I was admitted into the mental health ward and placed on oral tablets of olanzapine. But, even that, would not change the continued astral sex.

Whilst is hospital, I do not know who these men were that continued to stimulate my vagina and astrally have sex with me. I had to go for an MRI scan in the main hospital one morning, I think it was an MRI, and as I was being walked there by the nurse, I believed an intelligence agent was walking the other way to pass me in the hall and was smirking and smiling at me. It appeared this intelligence officer seemed to think that what I was going through was a joke. Something to laugh and smirk about.

I hated him for that. Of course, I cannot prove it was an intelligence agent. I guess it's just my delusion that it was.

This was my fourth major mental health hospital admission. The locked doors and hard plastic mattresses had become my home again. One patient was walking around with huge signs saying, 'Do not dehumanise us.' I thought it was a message to me. Another patient was also suffering from vaginal stimulation and was stamping her foot and crying. She was a sexual abuse survivor and I couldn't believe it was happening to her also. Some patients seemed like they were possessed by spirits, others seemed to be possessed by something demonic. I was possessed by intelligence agents and military personnel.

One patient I met had depression and used to do puzzles all day long. She was in a physical polyamorous relationship where, they have a partner but have relationships and sex with other men. She would talk to me of this and how she travelled to Melbourne and other places for sex and I felt like that's what these intelligence agencies and militaries wanted me to do. I hated it. I stopped talking to her. She was hospitalised and depressed from these polyamorous relationships and frankly, I just didn't want anything to do with it. Nonetheless, for me, the astral sexual exploitation would continue.

I had to meet with the psychiatrist once a week whilst I was in the mental institution. After a couple of weeks on my oral tablets of olanzapine, the psychiatrist asked me if "I could still feel the vaginal stimulation." I could, but it was less.

I texted my friend and asked her if I could go back to the apartment. She said no, so I had to work with the social worker in hospital to find a place to stay. I was now homeless. However, the social worker helped me and found me a room at a government community housing association in Turner in Canberra. I was very grateful for this as I did not want to sleep on the streets.

This housing association is like a community housing association that helps the disadvantaged or people on government benefits. It's an old building complex that has a series of flats with rooms to rent and communal areas like the kitchen, living room and a shower. The social worker took me to see it and I met with the Management Team who did the intake. I was very shocked when I first saw it. It was old, and I didn't like the idea of having to share with other women. There were only two female units and the rest were men's units. But I saw my room (room 10.2) and I accepted the placement.

She returned me to the mental health unit and there I met the psychiatrist again and told him I had found accommodation. He determined my release date and in October 2016, I was discharged from the mental health unit and moved into my room. I am forever grateful to the Management Team for helping me and providing me with accommodation. At least I was not homeless. This housing association had kept me from homelessness.

In my room was a bed, a desk and chair and a cupboard. I settled in with the one suitcase of cloths I had brought with me from the UK. There in my unit, I met another tenant who would become my friend and we would talk often. At night, she would lend me her computer, so I could watch movies which I got from the library.

I was still stuck (or what I call enslaved) in the astral field. Simon (or an intelligence agent) would visit me each day, and others, for astral sex. They (or the voices) asked me to stop taking my medication which I did. Each morning, Simon (or an intelligence agent) would make me meditate and from this I received much white light which I enjoyed. But I had no control over my body.

One morning, as I was meditating it was with someone from an air force. I do not know what air force it was. In this meditation, I would go through something like a portal of white light and be in space, in the cosmos. What appeared was Yoda (from *Start Wars*) and also a white alien with blue eyes. I was travelling in a spaceship with a pilot and the air force meditator said to me, "You need a pilot." The astral projector pretending to be Yoda would say, "Remember who you are."

I have to mention something here about intelligence agents, military personnel and political leaders is that when they project into the astral field, they can take on a character. For example, project as Yoda. Project as Ronald MacDonald or as an animal. To understand it more, you would have to ask them how they do that.

The mediation with air force person was very powerful. It was like a force and provided me with strength. What I didn't realise is that the meditation with this air force person would mean that an air force pilot would be the next man who would have astral sex with me, and I thought I fell in love with him.

Chapter Twenty-Seven
A Fighter Pilot from the Astral Field

As I sat in my bed watching a movie on the computer a fighter pilot would enter my body and have astral sex with me. He asked me (or the voice) to call him Dan and he would be with me for many weeks. He was also hypersexual and wanted astral sex a number of times a day. When he projected, it felt like he was really there. He would also make my legs shake from the energy and often the Yoda projector was there too. To me, I thought Simon (or another intelligence agent) was the Yoda projector.

When I was with Dan, I would also pick up that there was going to be a terrorist attack in Europe somewhere. I guess what some of these intelligence agents and military personnel thought was that I was clairvoyant. Also, with Dan, I would have thoughts that we would be married and have two children. All of these things he knew. The worst part about being with him was that I had phantom pregnancies. That part was disturbing. Dan also thought that the angel Tristan (who I call Tristin) was creating earthquakes on earth. That part is so hard to explain but when I thought I was conceiving an earthquake would happen.

I would walk around Canberra flapping my arms like I was an angel. During this time with Dan and the others I felt I was conceiving and bringing angles down to earth into other woman's bodies. I know it sounds insane, but that is what happened. I guess though, none of these spies will ever admit that.

When I was still with Dan and walking to the gym one morning, flapping my arms like an angel, a tall man wearing black shirt and trousers, who had sunglasses on, passed me on the street. The voice in my head said he was an intelligence agent and I should call him Wizard. Thus, I would call him Wizard. It would be a few months before he would have me too.

145

Each night with Dan I would get the computer from my friend and watch a movie. He told me that he could see me through the computer camera. I told him that was impossible because there is no Wi-Fi. Dan said, "I'm the military, I can see you." On these occasions, Dan would ask me to take my top off and lift my skirt up so he could see me naked. Then he would use some type of energy or astral field energy to stimulate my vagina and make it wet. I didn't think of it at the time, but I later became paranoid that perhaps Dan was filming me if he said he could see me when there was no Wi-Fi. This filming would also occur to me on the bus, with what seemed like a civilian who had broken the glass on his mobile phone, where these men would stimulate me and this young man on the bus would film me. I believe he was in his 20's. More sex tapes my paranoid mind thought.

One thing Dan kept showing me through the white light and portals was an alien species which were white with blue eyes. But I think this is just a projection. They were the same aliens I saw in the Yoda meditation with the air force guy. During that meditation, I said, that species must be destroyed. I mentioned this to Dan also. Little did I know this alien species, or what I call it's projection, would be with me throughout the next year.

Dan would pull my abdominal wall so hard through the astral field that it released energy up to my head and caused a white light flash across my brain. But it also caused a hernia and I went to the GP who sent me for an ultrasound. The hernia was about thirteen inches I think, and it is the only physical evidence I have that this was being done to me.

I asked Dan, through this brain chip and astral field, when we were going to meet. Little did I know I would never meet any of them in person. He told me to wait outside where I lived on a Tuesday and he would be there to pick me up. This was a lie, but I did wait outside for him and he never showed up. I felt utterly humiliated.

Other men would come in and have astral sex with me, merging with my body and pleasuring me. By December 2016, I had had enough. Although I have no idea who Dan is or what he looks like I thought I fell in love with him. His spirit, his energy, his sexuality and his love. To be honest, I fell in love with a lot of the men I was with astrally and it confused me how I could love so many men at the same time. But I guess you cannot call it love. You really can't.

After Dan did not show up to collect me, I lost my mental faculties and could only say three words at a time. The heartbreak of him not meeting me sent me into a tailspin. I thought by meeting him all this would stop. All I could do was mutter to myself, cry and scream at Simon (or intelligence agents) in my head, *why did you do it?* My brain was severely damaged from the lies and emotionally I could not comprehend how these men could do this to me. They seemed to be ruled by their sexuality. Having lost my mental faculties, I would wander around the streets of Canberra picking up cigarette butts and smoking them. I could not afford to buy tobacco or cigarettes, so I picked up ones from the street. I kept saying to myself over and over, *"Why did you do this to me?"* I don't think anyone much cared about what everyone did to me. It was then I thought perhaps some of these intelligence agents and military personnel were psychopaths.

All through Christmas and the New Year I was muttering to myself, having astral sex with men and falling to pieces. By January 2017, I had successfully got a contract of employment at a research organisation. God only knows how I achieved that.

One night, when I was visiting my friend at her place and she cooked me dinner, I sat down to watch a movie. It was then a military, I believe, put me in touch with some signal from outer space. It was a Light Force alien, although I thought another human species, and what she said to me was that there was 'danger in space' and that she 'loved me.' Then they put me in touch with another signal with another Light Force alien being and I would call him Charlie. He reached out his arm to me, he was wearing a space suit, and said, "Let's work together." I believe these Light Force species are in space to protect us, help us and work together with us. You must be thinking, oh goodness she is crazy! But I do not understand why humanity thinks we are alone in space. It's a bit like how, in history, we used to think the world was flat or that we could never fly aeroplanes. To me, we are not alone and there are both Light Force and other human beings in space and contact has already been made through these Illuminati Wizards and their clairvoyance. But I have to point out here, there are days when I believe in nothing. That Earth is alone in space. So, I'm a bit contradictory on the matter.

On New Year's 2016, as I stayed at my friend's place, I felt that many of the intelligence agencies, would put me through many intelligence tests. I felt like I was standing in front of something like a board room and I would sing to them and bring messages through from the spirit realm. This would go on for days and also when I started my contract work at the at research organisation. To reward me, these men would stimulate my vagina through the astral field to give me pleasure. Even when I was working, I would be put through intelligence tests and had to guess which intelligence agency it was and any messages about that intelligence agent. This went on and on for weeks.

On one occasion, the intelligence agent I call Wizard came in, held me in his lap with his arm around me. The message that came through for him and what I told him was 'you don't believe'. I have no idea what he does not believe in and his response was 'fuck.' Little did I know he would be the next man coming in.

Chapter Twenty-Eight
An Intelligence Agent Who I Called Wizard

It's March 2018. I sit outside the library (where I go each day to write) and I cry. I am smoking copious cigarettes. I am pining for an intelligence agent, who I call Wizard. I want to see him in person. Selfishly, I want him to comfort me and hold me in his lap (Wizards hold you in their lap like in that movie *Fifty Shades of Grey*). I want him to tell me, it's okay. I debate to myself whether I should take a bus over to where I, in my delusion, think he works and see if I can find him. I know the Police will arrest me if I do that. I'm confused and heartbroken. A man comes up to me and says, "Why are you crying?" He sits down next to me and asks me what is wrong. I cannot tell him. How can I explain all of this and all these Wizards and the astral field? I remain silent about it. Keeping the secrets for them. But secrets keep me sick. The man says he is from Tibet and talks to me of the cosmos, of enlightenment and of Buddhism. I sit there and think, but there are so many alien and human species in space. Through his words and kindness though I stop crying, I sit and listen as his soothing voice lulls me into acceptance, gratitude and love. So, I'll explain my time with an intelligence agent who I called Wizard, who I thought I fell in love with; in the astral field.

I think it was January 2017 when an intelligence agent I thought I saw on the street came in and had astral sex with me. He was obsessed with collecting intelligence about angels. Many angels appeared in the astral field (as I can see them and talk to them) and he asked me how many there were. I lied to him and said there was ten thousand. He also asked me if the angel Tristin was kneeling. I lied to him about that to and said he was. This intelligence agent would only stay with me for a few days. All he seemed to want was information about angels.

My days with the Wizard were interesting. Together I would have visualisations of us skinny dipping in Lake Geneva in Switzerland or kissing in Florence like in that movie *A Room with a View*. What was so different about the Wizard was that he was totally in service to his profession. He was so different than the others and he was a true intelligence agent. Needing and wanting information. But as I reflect upon him now, I know now he was totally cold-hearted and honestly didn't care at all what I was going through. Well that's what I thought. It took me a long time to realise that intelligence agents use astral sex to get information. I don't know why I didn't understand that at the time. I still think about the Wizard from time to time. Mainly nowadays I want to question him. Even now, two and a half years later.

Throughout this time, I was on a government benefit called Newstart. This government benefit gives you three hundred and fifty dollars a fortnight to live off. It's not easy. Part of the condition to receive the benefit is that you look for work and that is what I did. Once I started my contract at a research organisation, I thought my life would change. But each day I kept going through intelligence agency tests and clairvoyance readings. Alas, suffice to say, I wouldn't last long in that job either.

One morning when I was catching the bus to work which went via the different government buildings, I thought Simon passed the window seat I was sitting in, walking beside the bus. Of course, I cannot prove this but perhaps the intelligence agencies just used a look-alike. It freaked me out. I had become used to intelligence agencies using look-alikes on me.

During my contract employment at this research organisation, intelligence agencies would keep me in the astral field and ask me questions and do some type of astral field games and tests. They would also ask for messages from the spirit realm. Once, Simon (or an intelligence agent) and his team would try and catch me in the astral field and then tie me up and lie on top of me. Other times an intelligence agent would appear as an animal or in personas such as Ronald MacDonald and ask me to guess what intelligence agency they were from. They would do this every day and at night-time when I got home, these intelligence agencies would ask me questions and requests messages from the spirit realm. On and on it would go day and night.

One time, at lunchtime at work, I would go across to the mall and get something to eat and the whole place was covered with men wearing *Star Wars'* t-shirts and staring at me. It seemed to me that these intelligence agencies and militaries involved wanted me to win *Star Wars*. All I could think of myself was, why are they so incompetent that they cannot win *Star Wars* themselves? I was so angry one weekend sitting on the steps of the balcony at the government housing association flat, I screamed at these intelligence agents and militaries in my head saying, "I will give you *Star Wars*," and then the actress from *Start Wars* playing Princess Leah died.

It was during this time that I had the severe delusion that the brain chip in my head was hooked up to some computers and to an internet site where people could login. That I know is a delusion but it's what I felt. But I think that's what they made me think. Furthermore, when I would walk around the streets of Canberra men would look at me and smirk and smile. After I figured out that many people knew I said, "All Australian's can be charged with treason." The next morning people stopped looking at me and men stopped smirking. Was the brain chip linked up to an internet for people? I really want to know the answer to that. People could login and ask me questions. But I know that is not true. I know that is a severe delusion.

One night when Simon (or an intelligence agent) was in and having astral sex with me, I heard and saw, after I jumped out of bed, a man leaving one of my flat mate's rooms. I believe he was from a military somewhere. What had happened is that I was with Simon (or an intelligence agent) and talking about the dark force aliens and having astral sex. I believe the person in the room next door used some type of PSYOPs alien projection on me through a computer program and my brain chip. It was so ridiculous because the projection and computer program they used was of a black character from the movie *Monster's Inc.* That's what that man was doing next door. Just to terrorise me.

I had become completely fed-up and angry at these intelligence agencies and militaries and what they were doing to me. You see, during all this time, I kept picking up on dark force aliens and the danger that they are to humanity. In particular, I picked up a very dark force energy, which I called a blob, as it had not formed a life form yet. You must think I am crazy? But it confirmed what Annabelle, the Light Force alien had said, there is danger for us in space. But to be honest everyone, I just think they are technology projections. But I don't understand this technology.

What really pushed me over the edge was what I thought was a space agency. One night, they were mapping a galaxy and used my brain chip to do it. I don't even know how to explain that. But it happened. Then, in February 2017, the media reported that a space agency had mapped a galaxy and there may be alien life there.

At the beginning of February 2017, I decided that I would go back to England. At least there, I thought, they would take my brain chip out and stop what was happening. At least there I would be safe. Perhaps with it all, in my delusion, I finally thought the United Kingdom would deliver justice for me.

I went and saw the GP doctor and told him what was going on. He did nothing. I said, "So I am meant to kill myself for this to stop?" That night the Australian Federal Police came to my room and did a welfare check on me. A fat lot of good that did I thought. But I just lied to the Australian Federal Police and told them I was fine. They weren't going to stop me from returning to the UK.

I stopped going to work and went to Flight Centre and bought a ticket to London. I thought at least if I get to the UK this will stop and I would be safe.

I think it was the ninth of February that I flew out of Canberra on Singapore Airlines. Whilst I was at the airport waiting for the flight someone was on my brain chip and in the astral field asking me questions on how I was feeling. At this time, I was in a lot of pain on the right side of my brain and I kept being called 'delusional cunt.' That's when the *nasty voices* started. As I checked my watch, I realised I was running late and needed to board the flight. As I went through customs and security, I put my passport down in the tray, after I had gone through the security check, it was missing. The security man had hidden it in my handbag, but I didn't find it until I was going through the final security check.

I realised then that someone was trying to stop me from leaving the country. Luckily, I found my passport and boarded the flight to Singapore and then London. I wanted to go home to the UK.

Chapter Twenty-Nine
The UK and the Mental Health Hospital Again

The flight on Singapore Airlines was the most horrendous experience; as bad as my delusions about what I thought intelligence agencies and militaries did to my brain stem in 2010 with some type of weaponry. I was in severe pain on the right side of my brain and felt like I had leaking brain fluid. On top of that I had, what felt like, the military and intelligence agencies involved loading my brain chip which caused severe pain across my forehead. Furthermore, I felt I had millions of spirits attacking me or was it PSYOPs? In my delusion, I believed an intelligence agent, who I chose to call Scott, was with me the whole flight. I said to him, "I am not going to make it, I am in so much pain in my brain and I am going to die." He asked me to take the Mirtazapine I had with me and to "hold on." I did not sleep the entire flight. I believe he kept me alive and saved me.

When I arrived at Heathrow airport in London, I collected my suitcase and walked through Boarder Control and customs where I sat outside on the bench and smoked cigarettes. I had made it. I then went to the bus station as my plan was to catch a bus to Surrey and go to the mental health hospital. There I thought, they would believe me and would remove the brain chip and be able to help me.

One horrendous thing that happened on the flight and whilst I was on the bus is that I had voices telling me that my children and entire family had been murdered. I believed them, and it was insane to believe them, but I guess the play was to make me extremely terrified.

I arrived in Guildford, Surrey that night and walked from the bus station to the mental health hospital.

I arrived and went to the reception area of the hospital and asked to be admitted. They said, "We cannot take admissions it has to come through the Accident & Emergency." So, I left and caught a bus to Accident & Emergency. There I was admitted and had to wait for a mental health assessment. As I waited, I was in severe pain in my brain and also suffering from extreme anxiety. I didn't sleep. Voices, or what I thought was intelligence agencies kept asking me questions. They were ruthless, cruel and unyielding.

Eventually, the mental health team came and assessed me. I told them about the brain chip and the intelligence agencies. They said I would be going into the mental health unit again. I think it was the third day I was admitted onto one of the wards that dealt with Schizophrenia patients.

As I went to my room on the ward I lay down. I felt like the militaries were using some type of weaponry on my brain which was causing this severe pain. The pain would last for weeks. I couldn't sleep. I was so ill, and these intelligence agencies and militaries personnel were making it worse and they would not leave me alone. In my delusions, I thought perhaps it was some type of PSYOPs.

Every second of everyday I felt they tried to make me do clairvoyance. Why they thought I was clairvoyant, I do not know. They would ask me questions about global matters, and I felt like I had many people in the astral field and on the brain chip, even from West Africa. At night, when I tried to sleep, more people and voices would be asking me questions. I was not in control of my own body. My Schizophrenia had engulfed me.

They also told me this brain chip was connected to an internet that people could log onto and there were buttons on it that they could press that would cause pain in a part of my body. Personally, I could not even fathom if that was true as I cannot believe someone could be that cruel. To me it was insane, and I really was so very ill.

As they told me my children were dead (the voices), I did not email daughter for her fourteenth birthday. The hospital wrote to my mum who was shocked to see me in England and in hospital. She came to visit me and told me the children and the family were fine and everyone was alive. Another thing the voices would do is tell me that my parents are not my real parents and I was someone else's daughter.

They also did an MRI scan on me after I complained to the psychiatrist of a brain chip and severe brain pain, like I had leaking brain fluid. I never saw the results of this MRI scan, but the psychiatrist never told me that I had a brain chip. She said my MRI scan was fine.

Whilst I was in the mental health hospital, I would have many spirits visit me. In my delusion, I felt like one of them was Hitler. Hard to believe I know but I guess that is mental ill health. I felt Simon was in my body and on the brain chip the whole time and I started talking to him.

I even felt like I had Jesus Christ apparition in front of me and Prophet Mohammed talk to me. I felt like I had gone insane.

The psychiatrist started me on a drug called Risperidone which I cannot take as it makes me worse and also gives me lactating breasts. She then changed it to Abilify, which gave me severe anxiety and I would pace up and down the ward's halls. Severe anxiety is very debilitating. I went to the different classes and groups like psychology, art and mindfulness. In the psychology sessions, I would learn that I have to live with the voices but to me, I felt the assistant psychologist knew I had a brain chip. Frankly, I thought the psychiatrist knew too. Still I was unwell.

One morning, the voices I think, pretended to be my children. I cannot understand how cruel those voices were to me. Pretending that I was speaking to my children in the astral field and on the brain chip. I imagined I was talking to them about moving to Israel and asking them to come with me. They said no and that they didn't like me. The extreme mentally cruelty I was enduring was untenable.

I told the psychiatrist that I could no longer take the anti-psychotic she had me on, due to it causing severe anxiety, so I was switched to oral tablets of olanzapine. I have to say, that helped a little. I was in hospital for three months and got discharged I think in May. I moved into the assessment room in Hopewell House. There were seven other residents and they became my new friends.

Chapter Thirty
Supported Accommodation

Even though I was on anti-psychotics and anti-depressants, my delusions continued, and these intelligence agents and militaries would not leave me alone. You see, the medication does not stop them. They have to be stopped and my brain chip has to be removed. But the voices always say, "There will never be justice," and "You will always have the brain chip." The cover story for them is my mental ill health.

At this supported accommodation, basically a live-in mental health accommodation home, I met a support staff member called Clarisse, who I knew from my days at the mental health charity where I had therapy and took recovery sessions. It was wonderful to see her again and I was assigned a caseworker called Sandra. Basically, she was my point of contact and I would work with her on my recovery. I am very grateful for their assistance and how much they helped me with my recovery. But because I still had delusions that I was talking to intelligence agencies and militaries in the astral field and behind the brain chip, I wasn't recovering as quickly as I wanted too. Another geographical loomed in my mind – thinking this will stop if I move again.

On one occasion, I told the support staff that I was going to go back to Australia to live and that it was a mistake to be in England. But to me, intelligence agencies made me do that. I also told them about the brain chip, and I think all the staff there knew I had it. Even a friend, when I had lunch with her one day said, "You have a brain chip now." Admissions to me that it does exist.

I went to AA meetings during this time and also relapsed a couple of times. But, even in these AA meetings, the intelligence agencies and militaries would not leave me alone. It was also during this time that they would put me in touch with other planets and other species. To me, there are three other planets which they call the Light Forces. Annabelle's planet, Charlie's planet and Paul's planet. Each of these planets I have spoken too.

Other things that continued were being projected into terrorists in captivity by an intelligence agency. There these intelligence agents would want to know, via confirmation, if that person was a terrorist and if they would talk. This would happen late at night and they would keep me awake all night doing this. More astral sex happened with countless men. On and on, it would go every day. I cannot even write about it; it was so bad. I was just so ill.

On one occasion, these militaries and intelligence agents had me enslaved in the astral field and on top of earth. The energy was very bad and gave me anxiety. Someone who I called Tristin, took me into his arms. I said to him, "Why has God forsaken me?"

He said, "God has not forsaken you."

Yet again, in my delusions I believed that the intelligence agencies and military forced me to believe that if I go back to Australia, this will stop. They will remove the brain chip. I felt they were hassling me one time about the aliens with blue eyes and appeared to project them to me with others. This went on for days. Eventually, as I sat on the stairs outside and, I said in my delusion with an astrophysicist from a University (who seemed to be on my brain chip), these aliens will be destroyed in seven years. So much more happened, but I cannot be bothered to explain it. Often, I wonder if that was all PSYOPs. But really what I explain to you, as a psychiatrist would say, is what it's like to have Schizophrenia.

Since I had received some money back from my tax return, I went to my room and bought a ticket to Canberra, Australia. I lied to the staff at Hopewell House and told them I was going to stay with my dad and step-mum for the weekend. This would give me ample time to get on the plane. I emailed the government housing association in Canberra and asked them if they had a room I could rent, and they said yes but I needed to find somewhere to stay for one night. I packed a backpack with a few cloths and left early Saturday morning to get my flight. The voices would torture me the whole way to Heathrow Airport telling me I was Adolf Hitler's child. The extreme psychological abuse I felt the intelligence agencies and my voices were putting me through was untenable. But they didn't care.

I won't go into what happened on the flight home. More aliens basically and a bunch of other stuff. I just wanted to die. I do not want to live my life with a brain chip and with Schizophrenia.

Supported accommodation, as I found out from very angry and upset emails from my parents, called the police when I didn't appear, and the Police called Interpol. I know I stressed and upset my parents horrendously with leaving and lying to the staff, but I just couldn't continue living with this going on with intelligence agencies and their militaries.

When I arrived in Canberra, Australia, I went straight to the mental health unit and yet again complained about this brain chip and astral sex. I only stayed for two days and then moved into government housing association again. I am so grateful to the government housing management team for providing me with a room.

Settling into my room at this government housing association, I started to apply for jobs even though I had a medical certificate. In January 2018, I ended up getting a job with another consulting company, my third global consulting firm that I would work for. But I only lasted two weeks and I am sorry to this consulting company, that I couldn't do the job. I just could not function. To be honest, I didn't want to be in Australia and didn't want to work at that time. I needed more time to recover and get well and stable again.

I also relapsed with my drinking but managed to get myself back into AA eventually. Often, I feel though that either the intelligence agencies or the voices make me drink. Part of the powerlessness I have over my body.

I also went into a severe depressive episode and tried to commit suicide twice once, in February 2017, by overdosing on my medication. On this occasion, I was hospitalised for it. I saw the psychiatrist (well two different ones) and asked for an x-ray so I could see the x-ray film and have this brain chip taken out. But, they said, "No." They placed me on anti-psychotic injections instead of the oral tablets. I even emailed the End-of-Life Clinic in The Netherlands asking about assisted suicide.

However, that cost money. You see humanity, I don't want to live my life with a brain chip. Why is it you need access to my brain and my spirit? I was so angry at myself that my mental health was keeping me from living a wonderful life. I could not let my Schizoaffective Disorder win.

I knew I had to recover. Schizoaffective Disorder, both the Depression and Schizophrenia had me in its grasp and was tearing my world apart. I could not let it win. My shattered brain and all the experiences I had been through felt like I could not have a life. Not a life of quality anyway. The thought of that was intolerable.

In my last mental health hospital admission, I made a promise to myself that no matter what, no matter what was true or not, I had to recover and rebuild my life again. In February 2018, sipping coffee and sitting opposite the psychiatrist at the mental health hospital, he looked at me and said, "It's time to try anti-psychotic injections, Lara." He then asked me, "How do you feel about that?"

I said, "Okay." That afternoon as I sat watching TV on the ward, one of the mental health nurses came up to me and said, "It's time for your injection now." I followed three nurses into a consultation room which had a hospital bed and a sink. One of the nurses asked me to lie on my side and injected the drug Zyprexa into me, and thus a sort of journey into recovery began again.

On the last remaining days of this mental health hospital admission, I pondered about and planned how I would go about my recovery. So many of my friends did not even know I had Schizophrenia as I was ashamed of my mental health and what I had lost, my children, my career, my home. My friends were successful, living life to the full, with children and careers. I was on government benefits, living in government housing. A far cry from the day I stood in front of a prestigious British Girls' School and gave my Head of School speech. A far cry from the days at University where the world seemed like and oyster in my hand. Moreover, a far cry from the days I worked at a global consulting company and actually thought about becoming a Partner one day. Lastly, a far cry from being a good mother and being able to raise my children.

It is hard to piece together my experiences but month to month I had to work hard on my recovery. That I knew for sure. After a few months of the injections, what the psychiatrists call delusions; I no longer thought about (well except for the one about the brain chip). The voices sort of went; I was no longer in the astral field or so I felt. I was no longer in space. But still I longed for justice.

I still felt ashamed and shame is an awful experience. I had learnt and felt the mental health stigma and people treat you differently once they know you have Schizophrenia. I remembered that from the High Court of England in the custody battle over my children and the Court Clerk said to me, "Do you even understand why you are here." Some people treat you as if you are totally lacking in mental capacity. Well that's how I felt when she said that to me.

As I got released from hospital, I sat one early evening on the steps of this government housing association and thought to myself, I will write. I will write a book about my experiences and my journey with Schizoaffective Disorder. I will not live in my shame and embarrassment anymore. I will not continue to think of myself as defective. I will strive to achieve acceptance and recovery and I will be honest with my writing. Writing gave me an outlet. An honesty and the removal of secrecy. Somehow, I hope it will help others or even help those who have good mental health understand those of us with bad mental health experiences. Hopefully, it will help to tackle the mental health stigma.

But if I'm honest, I also wanted to write about the truth of what I believed has happened to me. The truth of my existence. More than anything though, besides the justice I yearned for, although I've let go of that now, is for my children to know, why they lost their mother.

Chapter Thirty-One
The Light and Recovery

It is September 2019. I am recovered but not cured as they say. I am stable. I can wear high heels again. I long to get back to work and have a job. I've returned to the UK to live. That's home for me. I don't belong in Australia and I'm so grateful to finally know that in my heart. Although I always think I did.

My daughter is connected with me on Facebook now and sent me a beautiful happy birthday message last year. I still have not Skyped with them. I did email my ex-husband and said I wanted to come and visit them, but he said no. I have not had any direct formal contact for five and a half years, he will not allow it. Five and a half years and I have not seen them. He will not send me photographs of them. I have no idea what my son looks like now. I accept this. That's just the way it is, and I am powerless over it.

I am no longer on injections and have oral medications to take instead. I worked hard over the last year on my recovery whilst I lived in Australia. Three times a week I used to go to the mental health hospital and do a range of therapies such as, hearing voices group with psychologists, art therapy, creative group and mindfulness. The staff there were great, although some of them looked at me with fear in their eyes. However, they helped me. I am grateful to them. I have had a clinical manager and a psychiatrist both of whom I have had great rapport with and whose encouragement helped me. I think the best recovery and therapies I have had were in the UK though. I use CBT a lot as a recovery therapy and I feel happy and stable now. I will continue to use CBT as a method of staying well throughout my lifetime.

I've been on a diet which has helped me lose nearly twelve kilos. I write, although my writing of this memoir has come to an end now. I am very hopeful about the future. The UK brings me hope. I wish to return to my career now. Well a career.

I read a book by Elyn Saks, Professor of Law, Psychology, and Psychiatry and the Behavioral Sciences at the University of Southern California Gould Law School, who wrote *The Center Cannot Hold*. It is a memoir of her journey with Schizophrenia and she is such a great writer! Her Schizophrenia is extremely different to mine, but I take great solace in reading other people's journey and recovery from mental ill health.

There's a Ted Talk by a UK psychiatrist, Eleanor Longden, called *The Voices in My Head*. In this Ted Talk she discusses how she hears voices and how her experiences have empowered her to live a life of quality, how to work with them and how, I believe as she mentioned in her Ted Talk, she lives happily even with mental illness.

I believe there is a life of quality to be lived even with Schizoaffective Disorder. I believe there is a career to be had, for me I'm going to return to work and continue writing also, and loving friendships and relationships to be found. I try and look back on aspects of my life with a compassionate heart, but I must be truthful, I struggle with that at times. I still hunger for the world to change and a part of me still hungers for justice.

I know my life and recovery is going well when I am operating from a position of kindness, forgiveness, love, gratitude and acceptance. That's my baseline and that's how I wish to try and live. I have to remind myself; I am not my illness nor my past.

I wish I could show you all this in a movie. It would be much easier, but I cannot. So, I hold the Light in front of me and continue my journey.